TO:

....

FROM:

....

DATE:

....

DAILY DEVOTIONAL MINUTES

for Women

365 Days *of* Inspiring Biblical Truth

JESSIE FIORITTO AND DONNA K. MALTESE

BARBOUR
PUBLISHING

Print ISBN 978-1-63609-667-4

Design: Greg Jackson, Thinkpen Design

Published by Barbour Publishing, Inc., 1810 Barbour Drive, Uhrichsville, Ohio 44683, www.barbourbooks.com

Our mission is to inspire the world with the life-changing message of the Bible.

Member of the
Evangelical Christian
Publishers Association

Printed in China.

INTRODUCTION

Beautiful soul, you are *never* alone. . .and you're *always* loved.

Wrap your heart in an abundance of reassuring truths and Bible promises as you read through these 365 days of encouraging devotions. Each turn of the page reveals an inspiring devotional minute (a devotion that can be read in just 60 seconds) alongside a related scripture selection and prayer starter, guaranteed to reassure and comfort your heart every day of the year.

Spend your daily quiet time with these devotions, where you'll encounter lovely blessings and the never-ending grace of your heavenly Creator.

Day 1

GOD CALLS YOU
AS HE SEES YOU

And the Angel of the Lord appeared to him and said to him,
The Lord is with you, you mighty man of [fearless] courage.
JUDGES 6:12 AMPC

Beautiful soul, never underestimate who you are. Never doubt how God sees you. Don't let your circumstances dictate your reality. "Go with the strength you have" (Judges 6:14 NLT), never doubting God's power within you.

When God calls you strong, don't think of yourself as weak. When God says you're found, don't see yourself as lost. When God sees you as worthy, don't think of yourself as worthless. Your strength lies in the God who sees you as you truly are: a mighty woman of courage, a beloved daughter through whom He conquers the world (see 1 John 5:4–5).

Help me to see myself as You see me, Lord.
I can do anything with You!

Day 2
I'M HIS

God's Message, the God who made you in the first place, Jacob,
the One who got you started, Israel: "Don't be afraid, I've redeemed
you. I've called your name. You're mine. When you're in over
your head, I'll be there with you. When you're in rough waters,
you will not go down. When you're between a rock and a hard
place, it won't be a dead end—because I am God, your personal
God, The Holy of Israel, your Savior. I paid a huge price for you:
all of Egypt, with rich Cush and Seba thrown in! That's how
much you mean to me! That's how much I love you! I'd sell off the
whole world to get you back, trade the creation just for you."
Isaiah 43:1–4 MSG

Sarah collapsed in tears. She'd scoured her house with the precision of a CSI team, but she finally had to admit that the pearl earrings her mother had given to her when she turned sixteen were gone. Her grandmother had given those pearls to her mother. And her mother had given them to her. Sarah's heart clenched in longing. She'd give anything to have them back.

God longs for you to be His with this same aching desire. You are a precious daughter to Him, and He would trade the world for you—in fact, He traded His Son.

God, You bought me at a dear cost—the highest price—the life
of another given for me. Thank You that I am Yours. Amen.

Day 3
GOD FIGHTS FOR YOU

"Do not fear or be dismayed because of this great
multitude, for the battle is not yours but God's."
2 CHRONICLES 20:15 NASB

Enemy armies were lining up to attack King Jehoshaphat. Terrified, he begged God for guidance. God spoke through the priest Jahaziel, telling Jehoshaphat not to be afraid or discouraged because the battle wasn't his but God's.

With this knowledge in hand and heart, Jehoshaphat led his people out *before his own army*, singing and praising the Lord! The story ends with the enemy armies attacking each other, leaving Jehoshaphat to simply pick up the spoils.

When multitudes are coming against you, there's no need to be fearful or discouraged. Simply keep your eyes on God, knowing He's got you. *He's* fighting your battles. Your job? To praise and follow Him.

Sometimes, Lord, I think my problems are greater than
You! Help me keep my eyes on You alone, to know You
have me covered. And all I have to do is praise!

Day 4
PLANTED BY THE RIVER

*His delight is in the law of the L*ORD*, and on his law he meditates*
day and night. He is like a tree planted by streams of water
that yields its fruit in its season, and its leaf does not wither.
PSALM 1:2–3 ESV

You're called to be like a flourishing tree. God didn't plant you here in this world so you could prosper only for yourself; He planted you here to benefit all those around you. He asks you to draw from the life-giving water of His Word every day and thrive in this dried-up, dying world. The lost and suffering around you will be drawn to the fruit of your fellowship with the Holy Spirit—your love, joy, peace, patience, kindness, goodness, faithfulness, gentleness, and self-control will draw them toward the living water of Jesus that sustains you.

Lord, teach me to drink deeply of Your Word and thrive. Amen.

GOD LOOKS OUT FOR YOU

The Angel of the Lord found her by a
spring of water in the wilderness.
<small>GENESIS 16:7 AMPC</small>

In the Old Testament, we find Sarah, who's frustrated that the baby God had promised to her and Abraham hasn't yet materialized. So she comes up with a plan: Abraham will sleep with her maid, Hagar. So Abraham lies with Hagar, who gets pregnant and assumes a sense of superiority over Sarah.

Sarah ends up sending Hagar away. But the angel of the Lord finds Hagar. He tells her to go back to her mistress—that he'll bless Hagar.

In response, Hagar says, "You are the God who sees me" (Genesis 16:13 NLT)

The point? Like Hagar, you're never alone. Your God is always looking out for you, ready to help, to guide, and to bless.

Thank You for always being with me,
Lord, even during wilderness moments.

Day 6
WHAT A GIRL WANTS

He withdrew from them about a stone's throw, and knelt down and prayed, saying, "Father, if you are willing, remove this cup from me. Nevertheless, not my will, but yours, be done." And there appeared to him an angel from heaven, strengthening him.
LUKE 22:41–43 ESV

As grown women, have we really changed much from our foot-stomping toddler selves? Or are we still demanding our own way? You might not yell with theatrical flair when you don't get your way, but does your prayer life reflect a total surrender to the one you belong to? Do you ask God only for what you want, or do you ask Him what He wants for you?

Today, tell God you're willing to forfeit your desires for His plans. He loves you passionately; and He, in His great wisdom, knows just what you need. Jesus was strengthened by an angel to carry out God's will. You too can receive supernatural power to live God's way.

Heavenly Father, help me unclench my fists and release my selfish desires. My life is Yours. In Jesus' name, amen.

Day 7
GOD EASES YOUR JOURNEY

He caused the storm to be still, so that the waves of the
sea were hushed. Then they were glad because they were
quiet, so He guided them to their desired haven.
PSALM 107:29–30 NASB

Read John 6:15–21. Jesus had just fed more than five thousand
people with five loaves of bread and two fish. Then He withdrew
to a hillside to pray.

Meanwhile, His disciples went down to the sea to row over
to Capernaum. It was dark, and the sea became rough and difficult to navigate. The men saw Jesus walking on the water and
became terrified.

Jesus said to them, It is I; be not afraid! . . .
Then they were quite willing and glad
for Him to come into the boat.
JOHN 6:20–21 AMPC

When you're in rough waters, invite Jesus into your boat.
He'll bring you to the place you were struggling to reach.

With You in my boat, Jesus, I no longer struggle,
for You whisk me to my desired haven.

Day 8

LINGER ON YOUR BLESSINGS

*The Lord is my chosen portion and my cup; you hold my
lot. The lines have fallen for me in pleasant places; indeed,
I have a beautiful inheritance. I bless the Lord who gives
me counsel; in the night also my heart instructs me.*
PSALM 16:5–7 ESV

Don't ever fall for the enemy's lies and then turn them into
complaints—that God is not good, that He doesn't care, that He's
abandoned us, that we deserve better, that God has taken good
things away from us. . .

What if, instead of focusing on our complaints, we looked
to Jesus, anticipating and believing that at this very moment He
is up to something *good* for us? Today, cultivate an anticipation
for where and how you will spend millions of years in the presence of God—apart from the enemy, without pain and suffering.
Because, friend, the lines have fallen in pleasant places for you!

*Jesus, thank You for Your unimaginably good plans
for me, for my beautiful inheritance. Amen.*

Day 9

GOD'S SPIRIT
STANDS WITH YOU

Be strong, alert, and courageous, all you people of the land,
says the Lord, and work! For I am with you, says the Lord of hosts.
. . . My Spirit stands and abides in the midst of you; fear not.
HAGGAI 2:4–5 AMPC

More than five hundred years before Christ was born, King Cyrus of Persia allowed the exiled Jews to return to Israel to rebuild the temple that had been destroyed. Two years later they began the work, but because of opposition from neighbors and the indifference by the Jews, they abandoned the effort. After sixteen years had passed, God spoke through the prophet Haggai, telling His people to be strong and not fear, to finish the work because He was with them, and His Spirit was standing in their midst.

When you're plagued with discouragement and others oppose your efforts, remember that God wants you to take His courage and strength and do the work He's given you to do.

Lord, when my spirit lags, keep me alert to the fact that Your
Spirit is with and in me. Give me the courage and the oomph
to do just what You want me to do. In Jesus' name, amen.

Day 10
NOT TOO FLAWED FOR USE

He said to me, "My grace is sufficient for you, for my power is made
perfect in weakness." Therefore I will boast all the more gladly of
my weaknesses, so that the power of Christ may rest upon me.
2 CORINTHIANS 12:9 ESV

Have you ever doubted God's ability to use you because of your
shortcomings? Throughout history God has been calling the
faithless, the flawed, and the broken to do big things for Him.
Despite your weakness, He is strong. Through your failure, He
is victorious. Trust that He can redeem every circumstance and
past experience in your life for His purposes. Wait patiently for
His timing, and see what He will do!

Heavenly Father, help me not to see my flaws as
stumbling blocks, and give me patience as You
season me for use in Your kingdom. Amen.

Day 11

GOD MEETS YOUR NEEDS

*"What I'm trying to do here is to get you to relax, to not be
so preoccupied with getting, so you can respond to God's
giving. . . . Steep your life in God-reality, God-initiative,
God-provisions. Don't worry about missing out. You'll
find all your everyday human concerns will be met."*
MATTHEW 6:32–33 MSG

Today, look at what God is doing around you. Before you step
into your home office, start cleaning the house, begin that long
commute, or wake up the kids—*stop*. Spend some time with God.
Open up His Book, ingest His words of wisdom, pray with all your
heart, and open yourself to His presence. Steep yourself in *His*
reality. See all that happens through *His* eyes.

Seek God's kingdom above and before all else, and you will
not only find Him meeting all your needs, but you'll find your
cup running over with blessings you never dreamed imaginable.

*I'm here, Lord, reading to steep myself in Your reality,
knowing You love me so much I will always have all I need!*

BLOOM WHERE
YOU'RE PLANTED

*"Build houses and live in them; plant gardens and eat their produce.
Take wives and have sons and daughters; take wives for your sons,
and give your daughters in marriage, that they may bear sons
and daughters; multiply there, and do not decrease. But seek the
welfare of the city where I have sent you into exile, and pray to the
Lord on its behalf, for in its welfare you will find your welfare."*
JEREMIAH 29:5–7 ESV

Can you imagine being carted off to slavery and God saying that
He wants to prosper you? He was telling the Israelites to plan
for their future in the face of their current hardship: "I know
the plans I have for you. . .plans to prosper you and not to harm
you, plans to give you hope and a future" (Jeremiah 29:11 NIV).

Jesus does the same for you. He enters your present circumstances and says that He wants you to dream here, to increase
and not decrease, to be a blessing to those around you. Live today
like you belong to the God of prosperity and hope!

*Lord, You placed me right here and now. Show me how
to bless the people I see today. In Jesus' name, amen.*

Day 13

GOD BUSIES HIMSELF
WITH YOUR EVERY STEP

The steps of a [good] man are directed and established by the
Lord when He delights in his way [and He busies Himself with
his every step]. Though he falls, he shall not be utterly cast down,
for the Lord grasps his hand in support and upholds him.
PSALM 37:23–24 AMPC

When you live a godly life—obeying God and His Word—God will not only direct your steps but will pave the way for you, busying Himself with every step you make! And when you're in that place, you can hear His voice behind you at every crossroad, saying, "This is the way; walk in it" (Isaiah 30:21 AMPC).

When you're that close to God, He's close to you so close that, even if you fall while on that God-directed path, whether it's because you hit an unexpected pothole or because you tripped up by momentarily veering away, He'll be there to grab you, pull you up, and get you back on your feet!

Lord, I want You to be delighted with where I'm going.
Help me begin by following Your will, way,
and Word, knowing You'll be blazing the trail before
me. All I have to do is follow Your love and light.

Day 14

CHOSEN

*You are the ones chosen by God, chosen for the high
calling of priestly work, chosen to be a holy people,
God's instruments to do his work and speak out for him,
to tell others of the night-and-day difference he made for you—
from nothing to something, from rejected to accepted.*
1 PETER 2:9–10 MSG

As humans we struggle with the insecurity of not belonging. Being left out. Uninvited. Unwanted. But beware of listening to the lies the enemy would whisper into your ear. Satan would love to cut you off from God's truth. Even if the people who should love you best have rejected you, you are never unwanted. Because God has chosen *you.*

Yes, you with your freckles or too-loud laugh or social awkwardness or whatever flaw you despise about yourself. You have been singled out and gently led into God's marvelous light of acceptance. He has a high calling for the life He designed you to live. And only you can live it as He planned.

*Father in heaven, I'm so grateful that I never have to fear
rejection from You. You love me better than any other. Amen.*

Day 15

GOD GIVES YOU SAFETY, SECURITY, AND GUIDANCE

I waited patiently for the LORD; and He inclined to me
and heard my cry. He brought me up out of the pit
of destruction, out of the miry clay, and He set my
feet upon a rock making my footsteps firm.
PSALM 40:1–2 NASB

Some days you may find yourself in a pit of despair. When you're in that dark place, wait patiently for God to draw you back out into His light. Expect Him to show up to save you. Cry out, knowing He *will* hear your voice and be there before you even utter your first word.

And when God gets there, He'll not only save you by pulling you out of the pit; He'll secure you by setting your feet on firm ground. Then He'll guide your next steps, ensuring they'll be steady and solid. Safety, security, and guidance from the Creator of the universe. . . What more could a woman need or want?

I'm overcome with peace, Lord, knowing You hear
my cry before it even reaches my lips. Thank You for
being my Savior, my security, and my guide!

Day 16
GLORIOUS LIVING

It's in Christ that we find out who we are and what
we are living for. Long before we first heard of Christ
and got our hopes up, he had his eye on us, had designs
on us for glorious living, part of the overall purpose
he is working out in everything and everyone.
EPHESIANS 1:11–12 MSG

Have you been living your life in a holding pattern? Are you waiting to discover God's greater purpose for your life—or worse, assuming you have none? Precious daughter of God, you were created with a purpose. God planned with skill and great attention to detail all the good works He intended for you to accomplish. Don't be distressed if you're living a garden-variety life—no earth-shattering fame or world-changing discovery in sight. What if your purpose is to simply love the next person that you meet? Or to encourage a neighbor or friend?

Wake up from your waiting! Today is the day that God has given you to do His work.

Lord, thank You for the designs You have on my life.
Help me to embrace each moment and walk in Your
Spirit every step I take. In Jesus' name, amen.

Day 17

GOD OPENS DOORS

"Keep on asking, and you will receive what you ask for. Keep on seeking, and you will find. Keep on knocking, and the door will be opened to you. For everyone who asks, receives. Everyone who seeks, finds. And to everyone who knocks, the door will be opened."
MATTHEW 7:7–8 NLT

Jesus tells you that just as a good parent gives her child what it asks for, knowing it will be good for her little one, "the God who conceived you in love" (Matthew 7:11 MSG) will be sure to give you what *you* desire. The thing is to keep on asking, and then keep on seeking that which you've asked for. At the same time, keep on knocking on God's door, expecting Him to open it to you!

The God who loves you *wants* you to actively come to Him. Never hesitate to ask Him for the things you need. Do not give up. Keep asking, seeking, and knocking. Father God is waiting to bless you.

Loving God, You're the one I can always count on to deliver what I need. Help me hone my desires, lining them up with Your will and way. Give me the patience and persistence I need to keep on coming to the one I can count on.

Day 18
ETERNALLY HIS

Then I saw a new heaven and a new earth, for the first heaven and the first earth had passed away, and the sea was no more. And I saw the holy city, new Jerusalem, coming down out of heaven from God, prepared as a bride adorned for her husband. And I heard a loud voice from the throne saying, "Behold, the dwelling place of God is with man. He will dwell with them, and they will be his people, and God himself will be with them as their God."
REVELATION 21:1–3 ESV

A new mother cuddles her swaddled newborn against her chest, a precious little life she gave birth to. Tiny fingers grasp her own, and she hopes never to be separated from her tiny bundle of happiness.

If you've never been embraced by the absolute love of an earthly parent, know that your heavenly Father adores you with openhearted devotion. He strolled in the garden with His first children, the masterpieces of His creation, and He also longs for your presence. His love for you is so great that He carefully crafted His plan so that you could join Him in eternity—never again to be parted.

Thank You, Jesus, for an eternal home with You. Amen.

Day 19
GOD GIVES YOU JUSTICE

Many crave and seek the ruler's favor, but the
wise man [waits] for justice from the Lord.
PROVERBS 29:26 AMPC

When things don't go your way, when someone or some institution blindsides you or unexpectedly pulls the rug out from under your feet, you may be thinking, *That's not fair!* But before you try to get some bigwig's attention so you can plead your case, why not take the wiser course? Take a breath. Wait for God to make things right. And, instead of holding a grudge, bless those who have harmed you. Leave everything in God's hands. Let Him be your guide. He loves you too much to ever steer you wrong.

Be a wise woman. Wait for God to make things right.

Lord, sometimes I find it difficult to wait for You to act. Give me
the patience to do so, knowing You're watching over me. You
want the best for me. And You'll make everything work out just
as You planned so I don't have to worry. I'll just wait. . .for You.

GOD OF THE IMPOSSIBLE

Your way, O God, is holy. What god is great like our God? You are the God who works wonders; you have made known your might among the peoples. You with your arm redeemed your people, the children of Jacob and Joseph. When the waters saw you, O God, when the waters saw you, they were afraid; indeed, the deep trembled. The clouds poured out water; the skies gave forth thunder; your arrows flashed on every side. The crash of your thunder was in the whirlwind; your lightnings lighted up the world; the earth trembled and shook. Your way was through the sea, your path through the great waters; yet your footprints were unseen. You led your people like a flock by the hand of Moses and Aaron.
PSALM 77:13–20 ESV

What worries for this day could possibly be bigger than our majestic and powerful God? Trapped against the Red Sea, the Israelites waited for Pharaoh's chariots to overtake them. Fear hijacked their emotions, and they could not see their escape. All hope vanished. But we belong to a mighty God who makes paths through great waters! He provides when our human eyes see only impossibility. Trust in Him today for the way through your troubles.

Lord, You alone work wonders in my life. Thank You for miraculous solutions. And even if I am not delivered from my trials, I know You will strengthen me with endurance to persevere. In Jesus' name, amen.

Day 21

GOD GIVES YOU A
SPIRIT OF POWER

*For God did not give us a spirit of timidity (of cowardice,
of craven and cringing and fawning fear), but [He has
given us a spirit] of power and of love and of calm and
well-balanced mind and discipline and self-control.*
2 TIMOTHY 1:7 AMPC

Your loving God has gifted you the spirit of power, giving you
the courage to face anything and everything in your life. And
His provision doesn't end there. He also gifts you the spirit of
love for Him, yourself, and others so you'll have the eagerness
to serve without fear. He gifts you with the spirit of calm so you
won't be steered wrong by your imagination, which may lead
you off course.

Today, spend some time meditating on your spirit of power,
love, and calm. Realize you have everything you need to do what
God has called you to do. . .and nothing at all to fear.

*I come to You, Lord, leaning into You, tapping into the spirit
of power, love, and calmness You have gifted me so I can
answer Your call, whatever it may be, wherever it may lead.*

Day 22
RECLAIMED

Therefore, if anyone is in Christ, he is a new creation. The old has passed away; behold, the new has come. All this is from God, who through Christ reconciled us to himself and gave us the ministry of reconciliation; that is, in Christ God was reconciling the world to himself, not counting their trespasses against them.
2 CORINTHIANS 5:17–19 ESV

Just as something beautiful can be crafted from the wood of an old barn on the verge of collapse, God can work this same regenerative creativity in your life. He can gather up all your broken pieces—the shards of your messed-up family, abuse, selfishness, loneliness, bitterness, and anger—and remake fresh your life that's breaking apart. He will give you a new purpose in Him and reconcile you to Him, the God who loves you. Come to Jesus. He will reclaim you from this world of sin.

*Heavenly Father, I'm not broken anymore!
You've taken me back and remade me in Jesus! Amen.*

Day 23

GOD'S PLAN FOR YOU

"I know what I'm doing. I have it all planned out—plans to take care of you, not abandon you, plans to give you the future you hope for."
JEREMIAH 29:11 MSG

No matter what's happening in your life, you need not feel as if God has left you to navigate this journey alone. Know that He has a master plan for you. And *even* if it looks as if things aren't going your way, relax. They're going *God's* way, according to His plan—which includes taking care of you and always being with you, working to give you the future you're hoping for.

So, although it's still good to make your plans, remember, God will have His way. And every way He chooses for you is the right one.

Thank You, God, for making me a part of Your master plan. I can relax knowing it's You who is in control. Show me what—if anything—You would have me do next.

Day 24

MADE FOR A BETTER PLACE

*God has made everything beautiful for its own time. He has
planted eternity in the human heart, but even so, people cannot
see the whole scope of God's work from beginning to end.*
ECCLESIASTES 3:11 NLT

Your heavenly Father planted eternity in your heart. He lovingly
kissed your soul with a yearning for Him so that you would
never be satisfied with less. Beloved of God, you were created
for eternity. The ache you feel is homesickness—the desire for
that breathtaking, everlasting land where the pain of this world
will ebb in the radiance of God's glory. A place where goodbye is
but a memory and sin is no more.

*God, thank You for the gnawing sense that there is something more
out there than this fleeting life. Forgive me for when I try to live
and move and be without You. In Jesus' precious name, amen.*

Day 25

GOD SHOWS YOU
HIS GOODNESS

*I would have despaired unless I had believed that I would
see the goodness of the LORD in the land of the living. Wait
for the LORD; be strong and let your heart take courage.*
PSALM 27:13–14 NASB

When life gets rough, when you're in crisis mode, when you see
no way out of the dark place you find yourself in, hang on to this
truth: you have a God who will show you His goodness in some
way in this life. He has things waiting for you, blessings that
are (or perhaps have already appeared) just around the corner.

For now, while you're in the midst of your trouble, let God
hide you "in His shelter; in the secret place of His tent. . .high
upon a rock" (Psalm 27:5 AMPC). Wait on God. Be strong and
have courage. There's nothing He won't do for you, no goodness
He'll not reveal in His time.

*I'm believing that I'll see Your goodness in my life, Lord.
So I'm taking heart while I wait in Your strength and love.*

Day 26

RUN FOR HIM

*But for this purpose I have raised you up, to show you my
power, so that my name may be proclaimed in all the earth.*
EXODUS 9:16 ESV

Eric Liddell won the gold medal in the 400-meter race at the
1924 Paris Olympic games. He refused to run in the heat for his
favored 100 meters because it was held on a Sunday. He broke
both the Olympic and world records with a time of 47.6 seconds.
Liddell went on to serve as a missionary in China. He lived to
bring God glory and to serve others.

You too were made for a purpose! God inscribed your passions
into the fibers of your soul. You bring Him glory when you take
up those passions and use them for His kingdom. He is delighted
when you run with perseverance the race He has given you.

*Lord, I give You my passions and my plans.
Use me for Your glory. Amen.*

Day 27

GOD GUARDS AND KEEPS YOU IN PERFECT PEACE

You will guard him and keep him in perfect and constant
peace whose mind [both its inclination and its character]
is stayed on You, because he commits himself to You,
leans on You, and hopes confidently in You.
ISAIAH 26:3 AMPC

God is not some distant spiritual entity that only checks on you once in a while. You're constantly on His mind. He's continually looking out for you, looking to see what you need, how He can help. As you lean into that knowledge and keep your eyes on Him, confident He will always be there, you cannot help but have that perfect calm. That's why, when bad news hits, you have no fear, for you are confidently trusting in the one who loves you like no other (see Psalm 112:7). Live in that peace. Love it. Cherish it. It's yours for the taking!

I'm setting my sights on You, Lord, trusting You for all.
Thank You for the perfect peace that gives me!

Day 28
ONLY GOOD GIFTS

Whatever is good and perfect is a gift coming down to us from God our Father, who created all the lights in the heavens. He never changes or casts a shifting shadow. He chose to give birth to us by giving us his true word. And we, out of all creation, became his prized possession.
JAMES 1:17–18 NLT

Our perspective can change when we see things in a different light. Activities that once seemed pleasurable and beneficial can often have dark side effects. That time we spend on social media can lead to toxic comparison and discontentment. That girl time with a friend may spiral into harsh gossip. Or that glossy red car could come with a monthly payment that strains your bank account. But we can live free of fear that God's gifts are anything but good. For He remains unchanged through the ages. He never casts a shifting shadow. And He has chosen to shower His goodness on you, His cherished possession.

Heavenly Father, thank You for Your rock-solid unchangeability. Amen.

GOD SHEPHERDS YOU

The Lord is my Shepherd [to feed, guide,
and shield me], I shall not lack.
PSALM 23:1 AMPC

There are no greater words than those of Psalm 23, which details all God does for you. He feeds, guides, and protects you. He makes you lie down in lush pastures, leading you beside the still waters so you can eat and drink and be refreshed in His presence. He restores you to yourself, leading you down the right paths—and all because He loves you just as you are!

Even when you feel as if you are walking in shadows, you need not fear, for the Great Shepherd is with you, protecting you with His rod and guiding you with His staff. He even prepares a banquet for you, anointing you with the oil of His Holy Spirit.

Thank You, Great Shepherd, for the tender
care You give me, Your daughter, Your lamb.

WHERE I BELONG

You are all children of God through faith in Christ Jesus.
And all who have been united with Christ in baptism have put
on Christ, like putting on new clothes. . . . And now that you
belong to Christ, you are the true children of Abraham. You are
his heirs, and God's promise to Abraham belongs to you.
GALATIANS 3:26–27, 29 NLT

Some of us come from families brimming with love and laughter while others' families are fraught with discord and tension. And some of us have no relatives at all. Unfortunately, we can't browse the world with a shopping cart and select our family like we do our favorite fruit from the supermarket, but we *can* choose God's!

Whether your earthly family is wonderful, lacking, or nonexistent, you gain a whole slew of new siblings through your faith in Jesus. And you become God's child, a daughter showered with unconditional love and acceptance—not to mention an unimaginably fantastic inheritance waiting for you in heaven.

Heavenly Father, thank You for
adopting me into Your family. Amen.

GOD HELPS AND SHIELDS YOU

*Our inner selves wait [earnestly] for the Lord; He is our Help
and our Shield. For in Him does our heart rejoice, because
we have trusted (relied on and been confident) in His holy
name. Let Your mercy and loving-kindness, O Lord, be upon
us, in proportion to our waiting and hoping for You.*
PSALM 33:20–22 AMPC

Focus on this: God's mercy, love, and kindness are constantly
upon you. And no matter how dark things may seem, your Creator is going to make something good come out of it. He's already
helping you to stand your ground. He's shielding you from all
evils—seen and unseen.

Your job is to trust God will not just bring you through
the stresses, trials, and temptations of your day, He will bring
you success *despite* them! Why? Because He's your help and your
shield. The more you trust in Him, the more you'll not just get
through life but find true life!

*Grow my trust in You, Lord, so that as my inner self
learns to wait and hope in You, I find myself pleasantly
overwhelmed by the expanse of Your love for me.*

Day 32
MY FOREVER HOME

But there's far more to life for us. We're citizens of high heaven!
We're waiting the arrival of the Savior, the Master, Jesus Christ,
who will transform our earthy bodies into glorious bodies like his own.
He'll make us beautiful and whole with the same powerful skill by
which he is putting everything as it should be, under and around him.
PHILIPPIANS 3:20–21 MSG

Friend, the struggles of this world are only temporary. Your true life is in heaven. We await its arrival with the same hopeful expectation of a mother-to-be. And when we enter its glorious perfection, the pains of this place will fade. Surely we'll be thinking, *I'm so glad that's over, and look what I have now!* We'll have, well, an *eternity* to enjoy the place where we belong.

Lord, strengthen me as I suffer through the pains of this
life right now, for You have promised that my homeland is
heaven! My experience there will so far surpass anything
I've known in this place! In Jesus' name, amen.

Day 33

GOD IS YOUR ARM OF STRENGTH AND PROTECTION

O Lord, be gracious to us; we have waited [expectantly] for You. Be the arm [of Your servants—their strength and defense] every morning, our salvation in the time of trouble.
ISAIAH 33:2 AMPC

Imagine living your life expecting this promise from God to become your reality. To awaken each morning, praying, "You, oh mighty God, will be my arm, my strength and defense," will not only give you the right mindset as you enter your day but will be a powerful tool throughout it. You can increase the power of this prayer by adding motions to it. Move your arms into a weight-lifting position when saying the word *strength*, and then swing them in front of your face in a boxing defensive position when you say "defense." Then go into your day with confidence, knowing God is with you and the fulfillment of His promise awaits you!

*Oh mighty God, be my arm, my strength,
and my defense every morning.*

Day 34

HIS COMFORTING PRESENCE

*"So do not fear, for I am with you; do not be dismayed,
for I am your God. I will strengthen you and help you;
I will uphold you with my righteous right hand."*
ISAIAH 41:10 NIV

As mature, sophisticated women, we would never fear a chilly, dark basement, right? But we do encounter lonely and scary places that can leave us feeling vulnerable and small—the loss of a job, the death of a spouse, an illness. . . And God promises to take your hand and wade into these deep waters with you. Are you trusting His strength to sustain you, or are you doubting His presence in your troubling circumstances? Don't waste another second on worry. Grab on to this truth today: God is with you!

*Heavenly Father, the enemy whispers that
I'm all alone. But I know the truth. In Your
presence I am never alone. In Jesus' name, amen.*

Day 35
GOD VALUES YOU

"What is the price of five sparrows—two copper coins?
Yet God does not forget a single one of them. And the very
hairs on your head are all numbered. So don't be afraid;
you are more valuable to God than a whole flock of sparrows."
LUKE 12:6–7 NLT

God is concerned with every detail about your life. He doesn't just keep track of your fingers and toes, but the number of hairs on your head!

Jesus wants you to know you have a Father God who loves you from the tip of your toes to the top of your head. Why? Because you were made in His image. You are His treasured companion and precious daughter. Just as God feeds the birds and tends the flowers, providing for them and helping them to grow, He's there for you, a woman so much more precious than any other creature on the earth.

Lord, I thank You for counting me
so worthy of Your love and care.

Day 36
SEEN

*Thereafter, Hagar used another name to refer
to the Lord, who had spoken to her.
She said, "You are the God who sees me."*
GENESIS 16:13 NLT

When the people closest to us are either spewing hurtful words or are so distracted that they seem blind to our existence, we can buy into the illusion that we are isolated and unlovable. But that lie comes straight from the deceptive tongue of the enemy. Beloved daughter, the truth is that you belong to a mighty yet gentle and tender Father in heaven. He is a God who sees you and every triumph and mishap and scratch and dent along the way. He misses nothing. And He cares deeply about you.

Lord God, thank You for seeing me. Amen.

GOD'S GOOD HAND
IS UPON YOU

*Upon him was the good hand of his God. For Ezra had prepared
and set his heart to seek the Law of the Lord [to inquire for it and
of it, to require and yearn for it], and to do. . . . I was strengthened
and encouraged, for the hand of the Lord my God was upon me.*
EZRA 7:9–10, 28 AMPC

Ezra sought God's Word with all of his heart! But he didn't stop
there. He actually lived his life by that Word, gaining the strength
and encouragement he needed to lead not only himself but
God's people back to the one from whom all good things flow.

That's a good formula for you to follow. Begin taking steps
today to prepare your heart, to focus your soul on looking into
God's Word. Yearn for it with all your heart, soul, and mind. Then
live by its precepts. Doing so will supply you with all the strength
and encouragement you need to triumph each day.

*I praise You and Your Word, Lord. It's water for
my spiritual thirst and food for my hungry soul.*

Day 38
JUST LIKE JESUS

Therefore be imitators of God, as beloved children.
And walk in love, as Christ loved us and gave himself
up for us, a fragrant offering and sacrifice to God.
EPHESIANS 5:1–2 ESV

Kids aren't the only experts at mimicry. Many of us adults are equally willing to do just about anything to be more like those we idolize—whether it's wearing the right clothes, living in the right neighborhood, or having the right job.

It's natural for children to want to be just like their parents when they're young. But who are you trying to follow? You are God's beloved child. Are you imitating His good character or looking to your fellow fallen humans for guidance and approval? Are you becoming more merciful, kind, generous, good, joyful, and humble? Are you emulating the sacrificial love of Jesus?

Father, I don't want to merely pay lip service to You.
I don't want to follow rules without having an inner
change. Make me more like You, Jesus. Show me
when I am only wearing a mask of love. Amen.

Day 39

GOD GIVES YOU REFUGE
UNDER HIS WINGS

"May the LORD repay you for what you have done.
May you be richly rewarded by the LORD, the God of Israel,
under whose wings you have come to take refuge."
RUTH 2:12 NIV

Because of her faithfulness to her mother-in-law, Naomi, and her trust in God, Ruth was richly rewarded by finding a godly husband in Boaz and through him, birthing Obed, who would become King David's grandfather.

Today, pause and consider under what or whose wings *you* have taken refuge. Hopefully, you've chosen God's. Make it clear in your mind and heart that if you put your trust in God, you'll be continually under His protection. And He'll reward you for your choice, just as He did Ruth and all His daughters who followed.

Your wings, Lord, are my refuge. I trust in You
to give me the loving shelter I crave. Amen.

Day 40

HOME IN HIS LOVE

"I've loved you the way my Father has loved me. Make yourselves at home in my love. If you keep my commands, you'll remain intimately at home in my love. That's what I've done—kept my Father's commands and made myself at home in his love."
JOHN 15:9–10 MSG

Jesus wants you to make yourself at home in His love. Come right in to stay. Get comfortable, put your feet up, and share everything with Him. He will treat you so well that you will know how to truly love others. Obedience is the key to remaining in His great love. "If you keep my commands, you will remain in my love, just as I have kept my Father's commands and remain in his love" (John 15:10 NIV). So regardless of what struggles you encounter today, conquer them from a place of rest in God's love.

Father, I want to remain in Your love forever. Help me to view my whole life through the lens of Your love. Amen.

Day 41

GOD'S WORD HEALS
AND RESCUES YOU

He sends forth His word and heals them and
rescues them from the pit and destruction.
PSALM 107:20 AMPC

When King Hezekiah became deathly ill, he prayed to God, reminding Him how he'd been devoted to Him and done good things in His sight. Then God spoke to him through the prophet Isaiah, saying, "I have heard your prayer, I have seen your tears; behold, I will heal you" (2 Kings 20:5 AMPC).

That promise—that God will send His Word to you to heal you and rescue you—still holds true today. Just believe that your heartfelt prayer will move God. His Word and promises are powerful and proven through the centuries.

I worship You, Lord, and adore Your Word.
With each passing day, increase my faith in the
power of my prayers and Your promises, to Your glory.

Day 42

KEEP ETERNITY IN MIND

*I am coming soon. Hold fast what you have,
so that no one may seize your crown.*
REVELATION 3:11 ESV

Have you thought about what your homecoming into God's kingdom might look like? Do you consider eternity at all as you go through the motions of your day? Beloved, our lives here are not without purpose. Someday you're going to be received into God's presence and welcomed to your forever home. What do you want that day to look like? Your labors, victories, and faithfulness today will determine your reception. Stay the course, soldier, to make it a joyous arrival!

*Father, I'm coming home someday! Give me courage under
fire in this battle zone. I can't wait to finally enter Your
presence and find rest from this war. I want so badly to hear
You say, "Well done, My daughter!" In Jesus' name, amen.*

Day 43

GOD BREAKS YOUR BONDS

He brought them out of darkness and the shadow of
death and broke apart the bonds that held them.
PSALM 107:14 AMPC

So many things can keep you in bondage physically, emotionally, mentally, and spiritually, whether they be addictions, bad habits, dark thoughts, or unseen forces. But you have a God who can break you free from whatever keeps you from living the life to which He has called you.

When you're in bondage, pray to God. Praise Him for "His mercy and loving-kindness" (Psalm 107:1 AMPC). Know He will bring you out of the darkness and into the light. He'll break whatever chains are holding you down, because there's no power greater than God's and His love for you.

Lord, break the chains that have brought me
down into the shadows. Lift me into the light
of Your freedom as I pray and praise You.

Day 44
THE STING OF JUDGMENT

So there is now no condemnation awaiting those who
belong to Christ Jesus. For the power of the life-giving
Spirit—and this power is mine through Christ Jesus—
has freed me from the vicious circle of sin and death.
ROMANS 8:1–2 TLB

You slide into a chair opposite your friend at your favorite coffee shop. It's been awhile since you were able to find time to connect. The tantalizing aroma wafts from your mug, and you feel the tension oozing from your muscles. Girl time and coffee, what could be more refreshing?

But then the conversation turns to the latest trouble you've been having with your daughter. And that's when you see it: the judgment. Ah, now you remember why it's been so long since you last saw her. . . .

Friend, you can walk away from the unwanted company of guilt and shame. Make a new friend! Jesus offers encouragement and forgiveness instead of condemnation!

Jesus, thank You for freeing me. Empower me
by the Holy Spirit to walk in freedom. Amen.

Day 45

GOD GRANTS YOU A GOOD NIGHT'S SLEEP

*In vain you rise early and stay up late, toiling for food
to eat—for he grants sleep to those he loves.*
PSALM 127:2 NIV

When you find yourself lying in bed at night, counting sheep instead of catching Z's, it's time to look at what's happening during your daytime hours. Are you anxious about your job or your duties at home? Are you burning the candle at both ends? Are you only conscious of God during morning devotions, or are you letting Him into every moment of your day?

When you put all your efforts into God's hands, trusting Him for the results and staying conscious of His presence, you'll find and receive the blessings He's pouring out twenty-four hours a day, seven days a week. Rest in God, knowing He'll take care of everything. Be assured He's got you—day and night.

*Keep me conscious of Your love and care day
and night, Lord. Grant me the sleep of Your peace.*

Day 46
A BEAUTIFUL SPIRIT

*Don't be concerned about the outward beauty of fancy hairstyles,
expensive jewelry, or beautiful clothes. You should clothe yourselves
instead with the beauty that comes from within, the unfading
beauty of a gentle and quiet spirit, which is so precious to God.*
1 PETER 3:3–4 NLT

As women, we often have a fascination for pretty wrapping, including our own. New clothes, a trendy haircut, and maybe a pedicure are just what the doctor ordered when we're feeling a little frumpy. But it's our spirits that are precious to God. A beautiful outside matters little to God if we're spewing poison from within. His desire for us is not flawless skin and a golden tan but rather the unfading radiance of a quiet and gentle spirit—a heart turned toward Him that chooses trust over panic and tenderness over harsh words.

*Father, teach me gentleness for those I encounter.
Whether it's my upset child or a difficult acquaintance,
may my response be beautiful in Your eyes. Amen.*

Day 47

GOD EMBRACES YOU

[I can feel] his left hand under my head
and his right hand embraces me!
SONG OF SOLOMON 2:6 AMPC

Slowly read the words above. Absorb them into your very being.

When stressed, lonely, and heartbroken, during those times when you feel unworthy or fearful, or even when just performing the most mundane task, stop. Go to the one who's waiting with open arms to receive you—just as you are. Go to the source of the love that never dies, that cannot be quenched (see Song of Solomon 8:7).

No matter what's happening in your present, constantly and consistently draw close to the one who whispers, "Arise, my darling, my beautiful one, come with me" (Song of Solomon 2:10 NIV). You'll find yourself at His side, imbued with His overwhelming love.

Oh my Shepherd, I feel Your presence. Thank You for these
words that bring me into the eternal reality of Your love.

Day 48

TEARS IN A BOTTLE

*You keep track of all my sorrows. You have
collected all my tears in your bottle. You have
recorded each one in your book.*

Psalm 56:8 NLT

Our response to our trials is usually "I want out. Make it stop, God!" But we also know that delivery from our trials is not always His answer. Because God is less concerned with removing our problems than He is with who we become because of them.

God is not blind to our pains here; they're real and they hurt. He sees every injury inflicted and records it for the day when He will return and everyone's truth will be told.

*Heavenly Father, my persistence and pain don't go
unnoticed by You. Your justice will reign in the end.
Mold me into a usable instrument for Your kingdom. Amen.*

Day 49

GOD SUPPLIES YOU WITH COURAGE

Do not be afraid of the enemy; [earnestly] remember
the Lord and imprint Him [on your minds], great and
terrible, and [take from Him courage to] fight.
NEHEMIAH 4:14 AMPC

Nehemiah led the third wave of exiled Israelites back to Jerusalem to rebuild the wall. Unfortunately, neighboring leaders openly objected. They tried to turn the Israelites against their leader and wrote a deceitful letter to the king to get him to override their efforts.

So Nehemiah prayed to God. He placed armed guards to protect those rebuilding the wall so their efforts would not be stayed. Then he told the people to take courage.

When others try to impede your efforts to do as God wills, pray to Him. Then bring to mind how great and awesome God's power is. Imprint your almighty God on your mind. And take from Him all the courage He's pouring out.

Lord, I'm imprinting You on my mind. Bring to my remembrance
all You've done for Your sons and daughters. Give me the
courage I need to follow You anywhere and everywhere!

Day 50

BREATHLESS ANTICIPATION

But as it is, they desire a better country, that is,
a heavenly one. Therefore God is not ashamed to be
called their God, for he has prepared for them a city.
HEBREWS 11:16 ESV

God is eagerly anticipating the day He will take our breath away
with what He's prepared for us in eternity. We can trust in His
great goodness and boundless creativity to come up with something wonderfully perfect—exactly what we've been waiting
for. Can't you just picture Jesus' excitement as He talked with
His best friends before He ascended into heaven? "I'm going to
get your new place ready, guys! It's going to be fantastic. I'll be
back soon to get you, and I can't wait to show you around! Don't
forget about Me!"

God, I can't wait for You to take my breath
away with my first glimpse of eternity. Amen.

Day 51
GOD LOVES YOU

We know (understand, recognize, are conscious of,
by observation and by experience) and believe (adhere to
and put faith in and rely on) the love God cherishes for us.
God is love, and he who dwells and continues in love dwells
and continues in God, and God dwells and continues in him.
1 JOHN 4:16 AMPC

The text above expands upon what it means to know and believe you're loved by God. For to know "the love God cherishes for" you is about *understanding* that God loves you so much He sent His only Son to give His life for you. It's about *recognizing* that love when you see it in action in your life or when you read about it in scripture. It's spending the moments of your day *being conscious* of that love, becoming aware of it continually pouring down upon you, by *observing* and *experiencing* its effect in your life.

God truly is love. And your job is to live in that love, to believe in, rely on, and lean into it.

Oh God, I praise and thank You for
the incomparable love that is You!

Day 52
PRAISE HIM!

As for me, I will always have hope; I will praise you more and more. My mouth will tell of your righteous deeds, of your saving acts all day long—though I know not how to relate them all.
PSALM 71:14–15 NIV

Too often we're totally entangled in problems.

Worrying about our problems.

Discussing our problems.

Thinking about our problems.

Pointing out other people's problems.

Our destructive thoughts are stuck on replay, and we seem to have forgotten how great God is.

Today choose praise over melancholy because, as the psalmist said, you always have hope! You are saved. You are redeemed. You are chosen. You are forgiven. You are loved so much! The more you notice all the little ways God cares for you, the deeper your love for Him will become.

Heavenly Father, I don't deserve any of this. What I really deserve is punishment, but You shower me with blessings instead. Thank You for caring about me, comforting me, saving me, and providing for me in countless ways every day. Amen.

Day 53

GOD'S WORD GIVES YOU LIGHT

The entrance and unfolding of Your words give light;
their unfolding gives understanding (discernment and
comprehension) to the simple. . . . Establish my steps
and direct them by [means of] Your word; let not
any iniquity have dominion over me.
PSALM 119:130, 133 AMPC

You're blessed because you have one of the greatest sources of power at your fingertips. The Bible—God's Word. But to access that power, you need to open its pages. You need to not just read it but to allow it to enter your very being. When you do, you'll find the light that will illuminate your path. You'll see things that were once unclear. You'll find the direction you need to steer clear of those things that will drag you down.

God's Word is here not only to guide you and direct your steps but to mold you into the woman God created you to be. Allow God and His Word to enter you and light your life.

Thank You, Lord, for the light of Your Word.
May it illuminate me without and within. Amen.

Day 54

A GOOD PLAN

*"For I know the plans I have for you," says the Lord.
"They are plans for good and not for disaster,
to give you a future and a hope."*
JEREMIAH 29:11 NLT

As Jesus followers, our hope for something better than we have here—an everlasting future with God in the eternal sunshine of His glory—should be a brilliant beacon that woos others out of the darkness to ask, "Why does your hope burn so brightly?"

God has great plans for you. Better than that, He has amazing plans for you. His Word is filled with the hope of your bright future. But we also live in the fallen world of "not yet." That means we won't experience all His promises in this life. So we live on a diet of faith and hope, walking faithfully in this world while expectantly waiting for the next.

God, thank You for Your good plans. Amen.

GOD ACHIEVES THE IMPOSSIBLE

The Lord said to Abraham, "Why did Sarah laugh?
Why did she say, 'Can an old woman like me have a baby?'
Is anything too hard for the Lord? I will return about
this time next year, and Sarah will have a son."
Genesis 18:13–14 nlt

When Sarah overheard God telling Abraham she would have a son, she laughed in disbelief at the impossibility, the ridiculousness of such a promise. After all, Abraham was nearing one hundred and she, ninety! So, she laughed!

It's hard to imagine someone that close to the Lord would have the audacity to disbelieve what He says. But the thing is, when you doubt God can do the impossible, *you* are reacting as Sarah did. Laughing at the prospect, denying His promises.

Make it your aim to take another tack. Do not laugh at God, but believe in and smile with assurance in His promises. When you do, you'll see them become your reality.

You are the Lord of the impossible. Help me to put my
faith in Your promises—for my benefit and Your glory!

Day 56
CHILD OF PROMISE

Therefore we do not lose heart. Though outwardly we are
wasting away, yet inwardly we are being renewed day by
day. For our light and momentary troubles are achieving
for us an eternal glory that far outweighs them all. So we fix
our eyes not on what is seen, but on what is unseen, since
what is seen is temporary, but what is unseen is eternal.
2 CORINTHIANS 4:16–18 NIV

Are you a glass half-empty or a glass half-full type of person? Paul
had the nerve to call our lives "light and momentary" troubles
because he guarded his perspective. He realized that he belonged to a God of promises and hope. But God doesn't promise
a struggle-free life. Do you need an overhaul today on how you
talk about your trials in this not-yet world?

Lord, I am Yours, and I trust in Your good promises. Amen.

GOD OPENS YOUR EYES

God opened Hagar's eyes, and she saw a well full of water.
She quickly filled her water container and gave the boy a drink.
GENESIS 21:19 NLT

After birthing her promised son, Isaac, through Abraham, Sarah told her husband to send the slave Hagar and her son, Ishmael (Abraham's first son), away. Abraham did, and soon Hagar lost her way in the wilderness. When she ran out of water, she and the boy sat down and began to cry.

God sent His angel, who said, "Do not be afraid! God has heard the boy crying as he lies there" (Genesis 21:17 NLT).

When you cry out to God, know that He hears you and that He's waiting for you to tell Him all your troubles. Then keep your ears open to hear His promises. Expect Him to open your eyes to what He has prepared to nourish you—mind, body, heart, spirit, and soul.

Thank You, God, for hearing my cries. Help me keep my ears
open to Your promises and my eyes open to Your provision.

Day 58
A FATHER'S LOVE

"My son, do not regard lightly the discipline of the Lord, nor be weary when reproved by him. For the Lord disciplines the one he loves, and chastises every son whom he receives." It is for discipline that you have to endure. God is treating you as sons. For what son is there whom his father does not discipline? . . . He disciplines us for our good, that we may share his holiness. For the moment all discipline seems painful rather than pleasant, but later it yields the peaceful fruit of righteousness to those who have been trained by it.
HEBREWS 12:5–7, 10–11 ESV

Satan would have you believe that God is punishing you or depriving you when you experience hard things in life. But the difference between discipline and punishment is in the intent. Punishment brings shame and pain, while discipline results in nurturing and training. God is not waiting to beat you with a stick when you mess up. Instead, He's looking out for your good! He loves you greatly and wants you to share in His holiness and grow in maturity.

And the best part is that God's discipline in your life proves your adoption as His child!

Heavenly Father, may I always remember
that You discipline those You love. Amen.

Day 59

GOD SUPPLIES ALL YOUR NEEDS

And this same God who takes care of me will
supply all your needs from his glorious riches,
which have been given to us in Christ Jesus.
PHILIPPIANS 4:19 NLT

When God told Abraham to sacrifice his one and only son, Abraham took the boy to Mount Moriah. There, just before Abraham was to kill Isaac, God spoke and stayed his hand. When Abraham looked up, he saw a ram caught in a thicket and sacrificed the animal in lieu of Isaac (see Genesis 22:14).

Thousands of years later, God would provide Jesus, the Lamb of God, to be sacrificed once to make peace for all with God.

Know this: God provides all you need. Rest easy in that knowledge. In Christ, you will never lack. God is always way ahead of you, preparing your supply before you even know you need it.

Yahweh-Yireh, I love that You're constantly
preparing what I'll need. Such love makes me
truly thankful to You, the source of my supply.

Day 60
I'M WITH HIM

*"Don't be afraid!" Elisha told him. "For there are more
on our side than on theirs!" Then Elisha prayed, "O Lord,
open his eyes and let him see!" The Lord opened the young
man's eyes, and when he looked up, he saw that the hillside
around Elisha was filled with horses and chariots of fire.*

2 Kings 6:16–17 nlt

A lone soldier stands motionless, relaxed and unconcerned as his
enemy attacks. And, just as it seems the enemy will sweep over
him with barely a break in their stride, a silhouette crests the
hill behind the soldier. And then another. And another—until an
army of thousands now stands behind the warrior. The cavalry
charge jerks to a standstill. With screams and snorts from their
animals, they flee.

You are not alone, beloved. Just as God didn't abandon Elisha to his enemies, heavenly armies with supernatural powers
stand behind you. Never fear in the face of terrifying spiritual
attack. God promises if you resist the devil that he will have no
recourse but to flee from you (see James 4:7).

*Heavenly Father, give me the strength to resist Satan's attacks
because I belong to the mighty army of the living God. Amen.*

GOD COMFORTS, ENCOURAGES, REFRESHES, AND CHEERS YOU

*God. . .comforts and encourages and refreshes
and cheers the depressed and the sinking.*
2 Corinthians 7:6 ampc

Where do you go when you need comfort? Who do you look for when you need encouragement? What refreshes your spirit? Who cheers you when you're sad? What do you reach out for or whom do you cling to when you feel you are sinking down into the abyss?

For a true remedy, there's only one place to go: God. Dig into Him and His Word. There you'll find the comfort that dries your eyes, the encouragement that helps you persevere, the water that refreshes, the cheer that reinvigorates, and the hope that lifts you up.

*God, when I need comfort, encouragement,
and cheering, lead me into Your Word. I'll then
watch for Your providence to raise me even further!*

Day 62
SACRED MOMENTS

So here's what I want you to do, God helping you: Take your
everyday, ordinary life—your sleeping, eating, going-to-work,
and walking-around life—and place it before God as an offering.
ROMANS 12:1 MSG

Holding a glowing candle in a hushed midnight Christmas Eve service or rising at daybreak on Easter Sunday—these moments feel sacred, reverent, worshipful. But what about today? What about today's laundry pile and stacked-up dishes? Shopping for groceries and paying bills? Sweeping floors and making dinner? Can these mundane activities be holy offerings to God as well?

Take back the minutes of your day. Reclaim them from the lie that nothing holy dwells in the many monotonous moments. Approach each task with an attitude of prayer, seeking God in each chore and knowing that you are exactly where you belong in this moment—exactly where He has placed you.

Lord, may I live each day, each hour, each minute for You.
Because each of my moments is part of Your story. Amen.

Day 63

GOD GIFTS ME WITH HIS PEACE

Peace I leave with you; My [own] peace I now give and bequeath to you. Not as the world gives do I give to you. Do not let your hearts be troubled, neither let them be afraid. [Stop allowing yourselves to be agitated and disturbed; and do not permit yourselves to be fearful and intimidated and cowardly and unsettled.]
JOHN 14:27 AMPC

Jesus has left you with His peace. His peace is not the peace of an unbelieving world, which brings no lasting good or real prosperity. It's the inner peace of which He is your only source. All you must do is not doubt that this peace is available to you. You need simply to take it up!

Jesus adds to the statement about His gift of peace by telling you to *stop allowing* yourself to be troubled, frustrated, perturbed, and disturbed. *Do not let yourself* live in fear, be intimidated, be afraid of your own shadow, or be anxious.

Accept the gift that keeps on giving. Take up the peace only Jesus can provide.

I revel in the gift of Your peace, Jesus.
Your very own peace has become mine.

Day 64
SAVED BY HIS LIFE

God shows his love for us in that while we were still sinners,
Christ died for us. Since, therefore, we have now been
justified by his blood, much more shall we be saved by him
from the wrath of God. For if while we were enemies we
were reconciled to God by the death of his Son, much more,
now that we are reconciled, shall we be saved by his life.
ROMANS 5:8–10 ESV

We serve an awesome God, who is capable of great power and demands justice from His wayward-hearted creations. Yet He withholds His wrath because He is also mercy—scandalous and unexpected mercy that is spurred on by a tender love.

God's thunderous display reminds of us His power, of our fearful position if we were to receive our due punishment. But then comes the gentle rain. He showers us with His mercy because of Jesus, who loves us and endured that storm of wrath for us—so that we could experience the life-giving rains of grace.

Thank You, Jesus. I cannot imagine what You endured
on that cross when You became sin and the sole focus
of God's mighty wrath. Thank You. Amen.

GOD GIVES YOU SUCCESS

He said to me, The Lord, in Whose presence I walk [habitually],
will send His Angel with you and prosper your way.
GENESIS 24:40 AMPC

Abraham sent his servant to find a wife for his son, Isaac, among his own people. Before the servant left, Abraham told him that God "will send His Angel before you, and you will take a wife from there for my son" (Genesis 24:7 AMPC).

The obedient and faithful servant went on his way. When he saw Rebekah, he watched and waited to see what God would reveal. When he realized she was the one God had appointed, he bowed down and worshipped the Lord (see Genesis 24:26).

When you're obedient to God, when you consistently walk in His presence, when you pause to pray to and praise Him, He will send His angel before you and prosper you on your way.

Lord, help me to walk with You in every aspect of
my journey, to obediently follow wherever You lead.

Day 66
REAL LIFE

He pointed out to me a river of pure Water of Life, clear as crystal,
flowing from the throne of God and the Lamb, coursing down the
center of the main street. On each side of the river grew Trees of
Life, bearing twelve crops of fruit, with a fresh crop each month;
the leaves were used for medicine to heal the nations. There shall
be nothing in the city that is evil; for the throne of God and of the
Lamb will be there, and his servants will worship him. And they
shall see his face; and his name shall be written on their foreheads.
And there will be no night there—no need for lamps or sun—for the
Lord God will be their light; and they shall reign forever and ever.
REVELATION 22:1–5 TLB

Eternity. It's brain-teasingly hard to imagine what it will be like
to live in God's heavenly city. We know that Jesus went to get our
digs all spiffed up for us, and we know that we're supposed to
anticipate the promise of this incredible place, but at the same
time we're left wondering, *What exactly am I supposed to be so excited
about?* We won't truly know until we arrive. But one thing is for
sure, God is not inviting you to an endless, boring sermon. He's
inviting you to real, beyond-your-imagination life!

Jesus, Thank You for the promise of new life. Show me how
to live for You here and now in my everyday life. Amen.

GOD WANTS YOU TO ABIDE IN HIM

Dwell in Me, and I will dwell in you. [Live in Me, and I will live in you.]. . . I am the Vine; you are the branches. Whoever lives in Me and I in him bears much (abundant) fruit. However, apart from Me [cut off from vital union with Me] you can do nothing.
JOHN 15:4–5 AMPC

Just as a branch cut off from the vine cannot grow or stand without the sap the vine provides, you, without living a life with Jesus, will have no strength to do what He's purposed you to do. Thus, you need to abide in Jesus, the Vine. Be united with Him by living a life of faith, dependent on Him alone, true to His commandments, and following His example.

As you live in Jesus, He will live in you. And there's no telling what you'll accomplish as you stay connected with the one who walks on water.

*Help me abide in You, Jesus, and bear the
fruit You've purposed me to bear for You.*

Day 68
CREATED FOR KINDNESS

"If anyone forces you to go one mile,
go with him two miles."
MATTHEW 5:41 ESV

Do you have a friend who always makes you feel like somebody special? Most of the time we just float through our day being nice to the people we meet. We ask them how they're doing to be polite, yet we don't really care. But kindness reaches out to lighten someone's load. Kindness sees a burden and offers to carry it for a while. The kindness of Jesus is irresistibly attractive. How can you become more like the one you belong to today?

Jesus, show me someone today who
needs my act of kindness. Amen.

GOD GRANTS
YOUR REQUESTS

*"If you abide in Me, and My words abide in you,
ask whatever you wish, and it will be done for you."*
JOHN 15:7 NASB

Jesus gives you two provisions to answered prayer. The first is to abide in Him, which means to have a vital union with Him, to live a life of faith following His example and His command to love God and love others as yourself (see Mark 12:30–31). The second is for Jesus' words to abide in you. When His words are living, at home, abiding within you, your thoughts will be transformed. They will become the thoughts that follow Jesus' lines of thinking. As you dwell in Him and His words dwell in you, you will begin to desire what God desires. You will be in alignment with His will. You will pray according to His words. And so your prayers will please Him.

*Jesus, may my desires become Yours as I abide in
You and Your words in me. To God's glory. Amen.*

Day 70
WHAT'S THE COST?

So that we would not be outwitted by Satan;
for we are not ignorant of his designs.
2 CORINTHIANS 2:11 ESV

If only we could clearly see the consequences for all of our choices. When we understand the price we'll pay for a poor choice, we make better ones! God has a good plan for your life, just as His Word promises. But Satan also has designs on you—and not for your benefit! Scripture says that he comes to steal and kill and destroy. When you face temptation this week, stop and ask yourself, *How much is this going to cost me?*

Heavenly Father, the plans You have for me are so much better than a momentary pleasure that will leave me filled with guilt and shame. Show me when I am being tempted. Amen.

Day 71

GOD HAS A PLACE FOR YOU

"My Father's house has many rooms; if that were not so,
would I have told you that I am going there to prepare a place
for you? And if I go and prepare a place for you, I will come back
and take you to be with me that you also may be where I am."
JOHN 14:2–3 NIV

Jesus has already gone ahead and prepared a place—just for you—in God's house.

Some scholars say God's house refers to heaven, that someday Jesus will return and take us all back with Him. Yet others think God's house refers to our dwelling place being with God now on earth and later in the heavenlies. That we attain that prepared place by loving Him and keeping His commandments.

Regardless of how you view today's verses, you can revel in the fact that God loves you so much He wants *you* to be with *Him*—forever and ever!

Lord, thank You for providing a
place for me with You. What love!

Day 72
THE BRAVE CHOICE

I eagerly expect and hope that I will in no way be ashamed,
but will have sufficient courage so that now as always Christ
will be exalted in my body, whether by life or by death.
PHILIPPIANS 1:20 NIV

The good Samaritan is often touted for his compassion. He had the courage to show kindness to someone who probably didn't like him back, maybe even hated him because of cultural bigotry. Have you been faced with a situation like this recently, one where you've had to decide if you were going to do the right thing regardless of whether it was popular, applauded, or even noticed? Take courage! Make the right choice!

Heavenly Father, guide me and lend me Your strength
through every choice I make today. May I remain
unstained by my decisions. In Jesus' name, amen.

GOD DIRECTS YOU

He will surely be gracious to you at the sound of your cry;
when He hears it, He will answer you. . . . And your ears will
hear a word behind you, saying, This is the way; walk in it,
when you turn to the right hand and when you turn to the left.
ISAIAH 30:19, 21 AMPC

Have you ever felt lost when you're on a road trip, even when you have a GPS? The good news is that, as a believer, you never need to feel lost on your spiritual journey. That's because God is your navigator. When He hears you cry out, He will answer you directly. If you obey Him, seek His wisdom, look for and expect His directions, you'll hear a voice, a whisper telling you, "Go this way. Walk in the path I have laid out before you. I am here to tell you whether you should go right or turn left."

What steps would You like me to take today, Lord? I'm listening.

CAST YOUR CARES

Cast all your anxiety on him because he cares for you.
1 PETER 5:7 NIV

Have you ever wondered, *Why am I so messed up? Why are my seams coming loose and my edges unraveling? Why does my anxiety flare over every minor hiccup in my day?*

There's hope for your anxious heart, sweet sister. It lies in trust. Cast all your cares that are rooted in distrust and unbelief on Christ. Your cares about your family. Your cares about your personal life. Your cares about work. Your cares for the present. Your cares for the future. Cast them *all* on the one whose shoulders really do carry the weight of the world. Trust that He is big enough, wise enough, and powerful enough to take on your cares. He is enough.

Lord, I'm done trying to control everything. I give all my fears to You. I trust You with the details of my life because I don't want to worry about them anymore. Amen.

Day 75

GOD GIVES YOU
THE KEY TO JOY

*"When you obey my commandments, you remain in my
love, just as I obey my Father's commandments and remain
in his love. I have told you these things so that you will
be filled with my joy. Yes, your joy will overflow!"*
JOHN 15:10–11 NLT

Jesus says that if you obey His commandments—loving God with
all your heart, soul, strength, and mind, and loving others as you
love yourself—and follow His path, you'll be living in His love.
That higher love knows no bounds and is yours for the taking.
And when you do, you'll be overflowing with joy!

If you're looking for joy—a deep-down happiness that's not
dependent on outward circumstances—follow God's commandments, Jesus' example, and the Holy Spirit's promptings. Then
you'll be on your way to obtaining and remaining in the spiritual
love and joy that never ends!

*Lord, help me to remain in Your Word, to obey Your
commands, to live my life as Jesus did, and to follow the
Spirit's promptings so that I may have the joy that overflows!*

Day 76

MY TRUE COUNTRY

"Lᴏʀᴅ, remind me how brief my time on earth will be.
Remind me that my days are numbered—how fleeting my life
is. . . ." We are merely moving shadows, and all our busy rushing
ends in nothing. We heap up wealth, not knowing who will spend
it. And so, Lord, where do I put my hope? My only hope is in you.
Pꜱᴀʟᴍ 39:4, 6–7 ɴʟᴛ

The things of this earth are a mirage or copy of what is to come. On our journey home, it's vital that we are neither unthankful for our blessings nor enthralled by them. The wrong perspective can lead you to empty pools of water. Be careful that you aren't seeking fulfillment, but instead pursue those things that have eternal value. Remember this life is short while eternity is long.

Father, renew my focus on heaven. Give me a
new desire for things with eternal value. Amen.

GOD ESTABLISHES
YOUR WORK

*And let the beauty and delightfulness and favor of the Lord
our God be upon us; confirm and establish the work of our
hands—yes, the work of our hands, confirm and establish it.*
PSALM 90:17 AMPC

When God gave Moses the instructions on how He wanted His
house (the tabernacle) built, He named two men—Bezalel and
Oholiab—as those whom He'd personally chosen and called to
be His craftsmen for the project. He filled them with the "Spirit
of God, with wisdom, with understanding, with knowledge and
with all kinds of skills" (Exodus 31:3 NIV).

Today, if you're looking for career advice or how to serve in
God's house, pray for God to confirm and establish your work.
Ask Him to reveal the talents He wants you to expend on His
behalf. Answer His call so that you can become His cocreator
as you build upon His beauty in this world.

*Reveal to me, Lord, what talents You would have me put my
hands to for You. Establish my work so I may answer Your call.*

HANDPICKED

Jesus said to her, "Everyone who drinks of this water will be thirsty again, but whoever drinks of the water that I will give him will never be thirsty again. The water that I will give him will become in him a spring of water welling up to eternal life."
JOHN 4:13–14 ESV

Friend, have you ever battled the feeling that you don't measure up, that no one wanted you? Have you ever felt like an outcast, searching for a place of acceptance and belonging? Jesus met just such a woman beside a well. She was looking for fulfillment but dying of thirst for something much more satisfying than what she was getting. He offered her Himself. He is the living water that fulfills our deepest longings.

Come to Jesus and drink of His message, and you will never again crave meaning from any other source. Not from friends or lovers. Not from the perfect number on a scale. Because God has handpicked you as His beloved daughter.

Lord, You have chosen me. I will never thirst for another. Amen.

Day 79

GOD IS YOUR
PERSONAL BRAVERY

The Lord God is my Strength, my personal bravery,
and my invincible army; He makes my feet like hinds'
feet and will make me to walk [not to stand still in terror,
but to walk] and make [spiritual] progress upon my high
places [of trouble, suffering, or responsibility]!
HABAKKUK 3:19 AMPC

God wants you to base your safety and hope not on blessings
that are temporary at best, but on God Himself (see Habakkuk
2:4). When you do, He will become your strength, your personal
army that can never be defeated. He will always protect you and
never retreat. With God in you and on your side, you will not be
frozen like a deer in the headlights, find yourself on the run, or
be shaking in your boots. Instead, He will be the strength that
empowers you to walk strong. He will lead you to the mountaintop of victory.

Be my strength and my power, Lord. Be my personal
bodyguard. With You in my heart, mind, spirit, and soul,
I know I can face anything—during good times and bad!

THE ENEMY'S PLANS

*Be alert and of sober mind. Your enemy the devil prowls
around like a roaring lion looking for someone to devour.*
1 PETER 5:8 NIV

Satan is one vicious foe. He's scheming right now to dangle desires in front of you that will make you want something that's outside of God's will for your life. If you are caught unaware by his traps, he will steal your joy, kill your hope, and destroy you. He's not above lying to you either. And the only way to fight back against his deception is with the truth. Read scripture daily, meditate on God's words, know His truth. Soak scripture into the fiber of your soul and wield it, like the razor-edged blade it is, to strike at your enemy. And the next time a hungry lion roars outside your tent, you can force him to turn tail and run with the powerful words of the almighty God.

*God, You have chosen me. But walking with You also means
being stalked by a lion. Make me aware of his schemes.
Give me wisdom and cunning. Bring Your truth to my
mind when I'm under attack. In Jesus' name, amen.*

Day 81

GOD IS FAITHFUL TO YOU

*So the Lord must wait for you to come to him so he can
show you his love and compassion. For the Lord is a
faithful God. Blessed are those who wait for his help.*
Isaiah 30:18 nlt

God promised Abraham that he would be the father of many
nations (see Genesis 12:1–3). But for years, Abraham and his
wife, Sarah, remained childless. Yet God continued to remind
Abraham he would have many descendants (see Genesis 13:16;
15:1–6; 17:6–7; 18:10).

Hebrews 6:15 (nlt) says, "Abraham waited patiently, and he
received what God had promised." God wants you to have that
same patience.

Are you waiting for God to work in a certain situation in your
life? Are you waiting for Him to come through on His promises?
If so, wait for Him. He's working behind the scenes to bring about
a blessing for you.

*Lord, I know You are a faithful God, true to all Your
promises. You love me and have compassion on me.
I take strength in this and await Your blessings!*

THE GLOW OF DAWN

"You will tell his people how to find salvation through forgiveness of their sins. All this will be because the mercy of our God is very tender, and heaven's dawn is about to break upon us, to give light to those who sit in darkness and death's shadow, and to guide us to the path of peace."
LUKE 1:77–79 TLB

Francis Scott Key was held captive aboard a ship in the harbor during the British bombardment of Fort McHenry. During the long, dark night, Key waited with expectation for the morning light. In the first ethereal glow of dawn, a flag snapped sharply in the coastal breeze. He strained to see, but the darkness shrouded its colors. The sun's first crimson fingers stretched across the waters and painted the land in glorious amber light. His heavy spirit was buoyed in victory. The Star-Spangled Banner still waved!

The banner of Christ's victory over sin will never be lowered. You no longer must tremble in the dark as you walk through this valley of the shadow of death. Heaven's dawn has broken! Salvation has come! His name is Jesus!

Father, thank You for Your saving grace. Amen.

Day 83

GOD IS YOUR HELP

I lift up my eyes to the mountains—where does my help come from? My help comes from the LORD, the Maker of heaven and earth. He will not let your foot slip— he who watches over you will not slumber.
PSALM 121:1–3 NIV

Isaiah warned against God's people looking to the power of men for help instead of to God. He wrote: "Woe to those who go down to Egypt for help, who rely on horses, who trust in the multitude of their chariots and in the great strength of their horsemen, but do not look to the Holy One of Israel, or seek help from the LORD" (Isaiah 31:1 NIV).

Look to God as the true source of your help. He—the Creator of heaven and earth—is watching over you day and night. Keep that in mind as you step in and out the door—today and every day!

I'm looking to You alone for my help, Lord!

Day 84
MY LIGHTHOUSE

Trust in the LORD with all your heart; do not depend on your own understanding. Seek his will in all you do, and he will show you which path to take.
PROVERBS 3:5–6 NLT

Friend, in this life it's going to rain. And it might not be a gentle spring drizzle. The winds might howl at you and threaten to break you apart on the jagged shores of illness, pain, loneliness, or poverty. But you belong to the Light. Hold on to your trust in Him with everything you've got, and He will lead you safely through.

Father, thank You for the guiding light of scripture. Amen.

Day 85

GOD REVEALS HIMSELF TO YOU

I have made Your Name known to them and revealed Your
character and Your very Self, and I will continue to make [You]
known, that the love which You have bestowed upon Me may be
in them [felt in their hearts] and that I [Myself] may be in them.
JOHN 17:26 AMPC

Do you sometimes wonder who God really is, what He's like?

To discover who your Lord and Creator is, look at Jesus. For He says, "Anyone who has seen Me has seen the Father" (John 14:9 AMPC).

Consider Jesus' love, how He heals, frees, teaches, and has compassion on all those He encounters. How He has not left you alone but has gifted you with the Holy Spirit, through whom He continues to nurture and care for you. How all this was done to show you who He and God are—love personified.

As you pray today, reflect upon the love that God showed for His one and only Son. Feel that love of God in your heart.

I come to You today, Lord, with a heart ready and willing
to receive Your love that I may know You even more.

HIS VERY OWN POSSESSION

*The grace of God has appeared that offers salvation to all people.
It teaches us to say "No" to ungodliness and worldly passions,
and to live self-controlled, upright and godly lives in this present
age, while we wait for the blessed hope—the appearing of the
glory of our great God and Savior, Jesus Christ, who gave himself
for us to redeem us from all wickedness and to purify for himself
a people that are his very own, eager to do what is good.*
TITUS 2:11–14 NIV

"Valerie won't come out with us anymore. She probably has to
go feed a homeless person or read her Bible. Isn't that right?"

Her friend's sharp sarcasm stung. She *had* changed since she
started taking her faith in Jesus more seriously. She had gotten so
fed up with the emptiness of her self-serving existence and had
finally realized that Jesus had already redeemed her from that
life. Now she was energized to do good things that pleased Him
by helping others. She was excited to belong to Jesus! And she'd
found joy in her new purpose by saying no to her sinful urges and
yes to His will. And one day He would be coming back for her!

*God, You've trained me to live a new life, a holy life
that pleases You. I've thrown off my old sinful habits
because I've realized who I belong to! Amen.*

GOD GIVES YOU ACCESS TO HIS HIGHER MIND

"For My thoughts are not your thoughts, nor are your ways My ways," declares the Lord. "For as the heavens are higher than the earth, so are My ways higher than your ways and My thoughts than your thoughts."
ISAIAH 55:8–9 NASB

God says His thoughts and ways are not your thoughts and ways. That's because His are so much higher than yours! So what's a woman to do? Rely on God's wisdom instead of your own to exchange your thoughts with His.

You don't need to understand His thoughts, His plans, His will, His words. Just obey them, even if they seem beyond your reasoning. Trust that He knows what He's doing, that He has something good in mind for you. His perspective is so much greater than your own. And His way is the best way.

Lord, sometimes my thoughts lead me astray. Help me replace my thoughts with Your words, and help me to do and be what You would have me do and be.

SURRENDER TO HIS WILL

*"Abba, Father, all things are possible for you. Remove this
cup from me. Yet not what I will, but what you will."*
MARK 14:36 ESV

Jesus felt the sting of faithless friends and sellout loved ones. On
the night before His crucifixion, Jesus washed Judas' feet and
shared dinner with him, and then Judas sold him out for money.
Later in the Garden of Gethsemane, while Jesus prayed through
the hardest, most rock-bottom night in His life in preparation
for a brutal death, all so His friends could be forgiven—His
disciples fell asleep.

Friends who've walked away. Spouses who've been unfaithful. Parents who've been abusive. Jesus understands exactly how
you feel. But He trusted God's plan. He forgave. And on the third
day He rose!

Let go of the pain of your past. Allow the healing love of Jesus
to wash over your rejection. You too will rise!

*God, not my will but Yours. I trust that
Your plan is good. In Jesus' name, amen.*

Day 89

GOD GUIDES YOU
DAY AND NIGHT

*God went ahead of them in a Pillar of Cloud during the
day to guide them on the way, and at night in a Pillar
of Fire to give them light. . . . The Pillar of Cloud by day
and the Pillar of Fire by night never left the people.*
EXODUS 13:21–22 MSG

When God's people were in bondage and cried out to Him for
help, He literally plagued the Egyptians who enslaved them.
When Pharaoh finally let the Israelites go, "God didn't lead them
by the road through the land of the Philistines, which was the
shortest route, for God thought, 'If the people encounter war,
they'll change their minds and go back to Egypt'" (Exodus 13:17
MSG). So He led them through the wilderness. And God never
left them. He guided them day and night toward the Red Sea,
which He eventually parted so the people could walk through
on dry land.

God's guiding you the same way. With God, you're never lost
in the dark but are continually guided by His loving presence.

*With You, Lord, I'm never lost. Thank You for
Your continual guidance down every road.*

Day 90

MY ROCK

*"I lay a stone in Zion, a tested stone, a precious
cornerstone for a sure foundation; the one who
relies on it will never be stricken with panic."*
ISAIAH 28:16 NIV

I don't want to follow a weak God. I don't want to worship a powerless being. I want to strut right up to the enemy like David did to Goliath and shout, "I come to you in the name of the LORD of hosts, the God of the armies of Israel, whom you have defied. This day the LORD will deliver you into my hand" (1 Samuel 17:45–46 ESV).

We worship a God who is all. He reigns supreme. He absorbed everything this world threw at Him and came out the victor. This is our God. He plans for an eternity, not mere days.

When Your enemies seem to be looming large, read this passage and remember, *I'm with Him.*

*Lord Jesus, what a mighty God I serve!
The woes and fears of this world crash and
shatter against You. What have I to fear? Amen.*

GOD ENCOURAGES AND STRENGTHENS YOU

*David was greatly distressed, for the men spoke of stoning
him because the souls of them all were bitterly grieved, each
man for his sons and daughters. But David encouraged
and strengthened himself in the Lord his God.*
1 SAMUEL 30:6 AMPC

While David and his men were away at war, the Amalekites made
a raid on their village. They'd not only burned it down but took
captive all the town's wives and children. When David and his
men came home, they wept until they had no more tears to shed.
Then the men talked of stoning David.

"But David encouraged and strengthened himself in the Lord"
through prayer. And God told him what to do. David followed
God's instructions and recovered not only all the townspeople
but their enemy's livestock as well.

There will be times of adversity during which the best and
only place to turn will be to God through prayer. He's the greatest
source of encouragement and strength you'll need.

*I'm encouraged and strengthened just by being in
Your presence, Lord. Thank You for always being there in the
darkest moments of my life and leading me to ultimate victory!*

TOO BUSY

*"I will arise and go to my father, and I will say to him,
'Father, I have sinned against heaven and before you. I am
no longer worthy to be called your son. Treat me as one of
your hired servants.' And he arose and came to his father.
But while he was still a long way off, his father saw him and felt
compassion, and ran and embraced him and kissed him."*

LUKE 15:18–20 ESV

Dorothy scribbled in the last letter of her crossword puzzle
and sighed. It was her third puzzle of the day. She glanced at
the silent phone beside her chair. Her children were thriving.
But they didn't seem to have a moment to spare for a chat with
their mother anymore. Tomorrow, yes, maybe tomorrow they
would call.

Have you been neglecting your heavenly Father? He waits for
you to open the line and take a time-out from your schedule to
spend quality time with Him. Just like the father of the prodigal
son, He's overjoyed when you come. Spend some time with Him
in prayer right now.

*Heavenly Father, I'm so sorry when I rush through
my day without talking to You. Renew my thirst
for Your Word. In Jesus' name, amen.*

GOD'S SPIRIT PRAYS FOR YOU

We don't know what God wants us to pray for. But the
Holy Spirit prays for us with groanings that cannot be
expressed in words. And the Father who knows all hearts
knows what the Spirit is saying, for the Spirit pleads
for us believers in harmony with God's own will.
ROMANS 8:26–27 NLT

At times situations can be so complicated that you might not know exactly how to pray. Or your heart is so wounded that you cannot find the words to say to God. The wonder of all this is that God has given you the Holy Spirit. He will pray for you for those things that you cannot express in words. He will translate your moans, groans, and sighs to God. And the Father, who knows your heart like no other, will understand what the Spirit is saying.

The Spirit will then guide you into God's Word, showing you what you need to know and giving you the power to apply that wisdom to your life—keeping you in the blessed harmony with God and what He has planned for you!

Thank You, Spirit, for always being there for me,
being my translator, comforter, and guide.

Day 94

A NEW ATTITUDE

Throw off your old sinful nature and your former way of life,
which is corrupted by lust and deception. Instead, let the
Spirit renew your thoughts and attitudes. Put on your new
nature, created to be like God—truly righteous and holy.
EPHESIANS 4:22–24 NLT

Maggie loved her grandmother's four-poster cherry bed. But the finish was cracked and weathered. So she began the painstaking process of stripping off the old finish. She carefully scraped off layer after gunky layer of ruined varnish. It was a messy job. But in the end her grandmother's bed was more beautiful than ever.

Have you begun the hard process of stripping off your old layers of sin? Have your life habits changed since you met Jesus? When we belong to Him, He calls us into a new life. Those old corrupted habits will chain you in darkness. Allow Him to give you a new attitude for your mind—one that seeks His kingdom.

Jesus, I was burned out and defeated. But through Your strength
I began to change. One false belief, sinful habit, and wrong
attitude at a time, You scraped off the ravages of my former
ways until I began to look more like Your Son. Thank You,
Jesus, that I live in newness and life! In Your name, amen.

Day 95

GOD STICKS WITH YOU

"I am with you, and I will protect you wherever you go.
One day I will bring you back to this land. I will not leave you
until I have finished giving you everything I have promised
you." Then Jacob awoke from his sleep and said, "Surely
the Lord is in this place, and I wasn't even aware of it!"
GENESIS 28:15–16 NLT

Having deceived his brother and father, Jacob was on the run. He slept under the stars, using a rock as a pillow. He dreamed of a ladder between heaven and earth. God stood at the top as His angels ascended and descended upon it.

Toward the end of his dream, Jacob heard God's promise that He'd always be with him, protecting him and never leaving him until Jacob had received all God promised him.

No matter what you're going through, God is with you. Even during the hardest trials, He's looking out for you, protecting you, sticking with you until all His promises to you are fulfilled. You don't need to wonder. God will never leave you!

Lord, thank You for sticking with me through thick and thin.
Help me to be continually aware of Your presence at my side!

INTERRUPTED

*As Jesus was on his way. . .a woman was there
who had been subject to bleeding for twelve years. . . .
She came up behind him and touched the edge of
his cloak, and immediately her bleeding stopped.*

LUKE 8:42–44 NIV

How do you normally react to unscheduled events that threaten to derail your daily plans? The Bible is filled with stories of Jesus being interrupted. And many of these stories involve miraculous happenings. While He was traveling from place to place, a woman reached out and touched Him. Jesus stopped and healed her.

Don't overlook the unrehearsed, interrupted moments of your life. God is at work in the in-between. When you're interrupted today, pause and look for God's movements.

Jesus, help me to stop and see Your work around me. Amen.

Day 97

GOD BREAKS
THROUGH FOR YOU

*So [Israel] came up to Baal-perazim, and David smote [the
Philistines] there. Then David said, God has broken my enemies
by my hand, like the bursting forth of waters. Therefore they called
the name of that place Baal-perazim [Lord of breaking through].*
1 CHRONICLES 14:11 AMPC

When the Philistines heard that David had been anointed king
over Israel, they decided to challenge him. David's first response
was to ask the Lord if he should go up against them and, if he
did, would God give them into his hand. God told David to go.
He would give him victory.

David followed God's instructions. Because David earnestly
sought God, listened to Him, then followed His guidance, God
gave him many breakthroughs.

When you're looking for a breakthrough, instead of attempt-
ing to achieve one in your own power and wisdom, seek God.
Listen to what He has to say, and then follow His wisdom, being
patient for Him to work things out His way.

*Lord, I need a breakthrough, so I'm seeking Your face,
listening for Your guidance, ready to obey.*

UNDER HIS WINGS

*"O Jerusalem, Jerusalem, the city that kills the prophets
and stones God's messengers! How often I have wanted
to gather your children together as a hen protects her
chicks beneath her wings, but you wouldn't let me."*
LUKE 13:34 NLT

Imagine that tomorrow is your baby daughter's first day of kindergarten. You swipe a stray tear as you make an extra sandwich and pack an extra lunch box this year. You look forward to the joy and excitement of new school memories but mourn the loss of your baby as she grows into a big girl. When she comes bounding into the kitchen to show you her outfit for tomorrow, you pull her into a tight hug. You just can't hold her close enough.

Your heavenly Father feels this same deep love for you. He wants to gather you in because He loves you tenderly. He showers you with outlandish gifts of grace, mercy, belonging, and acceptance. And most of all, love.

*Lord, show me when I'm pulling away from You. I don't want to
be separated from Your amazing love. Gather me in, right under
Your protective wings. And hold me near. In Jesus' name, amen.*

GOD PROSPERS THE WORK OF YOUR HANDS

But the Lord was with Joseph, and he [though a slave]
was a successful and prosperous man. . . . And his master
saw that the Lord was with him and that the Lord made
all that he did to flourish and succeed in his hand.

GENESIS 39:2–3 AMPC

Joseph had a rough span of about twelve years. First his jealous brothers stuck him in a pit, and then they sold him to traders. He landed as a slave to an Egyptian and was imprisoned based on false accusations from his master's wife.

Yet, no matter what happened to him, Joseph never blamed God for his circumstances. He never stopped trusting that God would help him. He continued to serve the Lord from wherever he landed. Because of all these things, God prospered whatever Joseph put his hand to—and people noticed!

Whatever work came to Joseph, he did it the best that he could, trusting God to give him wisdom and guidance where needed. As you do the same, God will prosper you and those whose lives you touch!

I'm trusting You, Lord, to help me do
the best work I can—for You and others!

Day 100
A DROP OF MERCY

*"Blessed [content, sheltered by God's promises]
are the merciful, for they will receive mercy."*
MATTHEW 5:7 AMP

You hear the angry man berating the waitress for his cold coffee at the table behind you. The poor woman looks ready to snap. She snatches his coffee mug from the table and stomps off to the kitchen.

The frazzled waitress returns to plop his steaming coffee down in front of him, rattling his silverware as she does. Then she steps over to your table and turns her scowl on you.

What should you do? How would Jesus react in this moment?

All it takes is a pinch of mercy and grace to change the course of someone's day. Someone around you needs a drop of mercy. Reflect the beautiful love and mercy of Jesus to them.

*God, You are a gracious and merciful God. You have shown
me lavish mercy that I don't deserve. Because I belong to
You, how could I do anything other than scatter Your mercy
onto all those around me. Show me someone today who
needs an extra helping of mercy. In Jesus' name, amen.*

GOD IS IN CONTROL OF YOUR CIRCUMSTANCES

*"So it was God who sent me here, not you! . . . You intended
to harm me, but God intended it all for good. He brought me
to this position so I could save the lives of many people."*
GENESIS 45:8; 50:20 NLT

Joseph trusted God while learning valuable lessons every step
of the way. One day, he was sent to interpret Pharaoh's dreams.
The leader of Egypt, impressed with Joseph, made him lord of
his household and ruler over the land.

It was his high-ranking position in Egypt that enabled
Joseph to be able to save the lives of his father and his brothers'
families. And it was his trust that God was in control all the
time that allowed him to forgive them. Joseph realized that it
was God who had worked this plan!

Rest easy. Know God is in control. He will make all things
come out for good if you will just trust Him, be patient, and
keep your faith.

*What a relief, Lord, to know You are always working out my
circumstance for good. Thank You for always being with me!*

Day 102
RADIANT

*When Moses came down from Mount Sinai carrying the
two Tablets of The Testimony, he didn't know that the skin
of his face glowed because he had been speaking with GOD.*
EXODUS 34:29 MSG

As believers in Jesus, we can reflect His light into this dark world
that's been overtaken by sin and despair. The more time you
spend getting to know God by reading His Word, praying about
His desires for your life, praising Him for His goodness, and being
still before Him, the more radiant you will become.

What's in your heart will show on your face! Your countenance will glow with the peace and joy of resting in His promises,
trusting in His goodness, and basking in His grace.

*Heavenly Father, in Your presence is where I belong.
I love being with You both in the quiet and the busyness
of my days. I long for the time when I will dwell in
the sunshine of Your glory forever. Amen.*

GOD PROVIDES YOUR "NEVERTHELESS"

The king and his men marched to Jerusalem to attack the Jebusites,
who lived there. The Jebusites said to David, "You will not get
in here; even the blind and the lame can ward you off." They
thought, "David cannot get in here." Nevertheless, David
captured the fortress of Zion—which is the City of David.
2 SAMUEL 5:6–7 NIV (EMPHASIS ADDED)

When David became king over all Israel, he and his men marched to Jerusalem to attack the people who lived there. But the inhabitants taunted David, disparaging his strength and vowing he would never be able to even get into the city. But because David walked closely with, consulted with, and obeyed God, he did indeed capture the city and made it his stronghold from which he would rule over God's people.

When you walk closely with God, asking for His guidance at every crossroad and following Him with all your heart as did David, you too can count on God providing you with a "nevertheless," no matter how daunting the challenge. Nothing is impossible with God!

I want to walk so closely with You, Lord, that I no
longer know where I end and You begin. With You
I know no challenge can stand in our way!

Day 104

BIGGER PLANS

Now may the God of peace who brought again from the dead our Lord Jesus, the great shepherd of the sheep, by the blood of the eternal covenant, equip you with everything good that you may do his will, working in us that which is pleasing in his sight, through Jesus Christ.
HEBREWS 13:20–21 ESV

The disciples were hiding in the upper room with the door barred. Fear plagued them. Doubts tormented their minds. Their world seemed to be crumbling just when things had been going along so well. Jesus was dead. Buried in a borrowed tomb. . .

Then Jesus was there! *Alive!* Joy accosted them as they began to grasp God's plan: a Savior for not only this life but the next. Forgiveness for sins and a new covenant of grace. A kingdom not of this world.

Sometimes we miss God's movement, His plans, His provision, His hope. Are you locked in an upper room bound in fear? Ask Jesus to join you there and strengthen your faith. Ask Him for the next step in His plans for you.

Jesus, sometimes I miss what You're doing because I'm looking with earthly eyes. Open my spiritual eyes to Your plans for me. Amen.

GOD GIVES YOU ASSURANCE TO GO FORWARD

*She said, "It will be well." Then she saddled a donkey and said
to her servant, "Drive and go forward; do not slow down."*
2 KINGS 4:23–24 NASB

A childless Shunamite woman made a room in her house for the prophet Elijah to stay in whenever he came to town. In return for her hospitality, Elijah said she'd have a son the coming spring. And she did! But several years later, her son died. She told her husband she was going to see the man of God. He asked her why, and she replied, "It will be well."

When she came face-to-face with Elijah, she was in obvious distress. Elijah raised the boy from the dead and returned him to his mother's arms.

This Shunamite woman remained calm because she knew that with God, all would be well. May you move forward with such positive faith no matter what life brings!

With You, God, I know all will be well.

LIVE GENEROUSLY!

*"Whoever wants to be great must become a servant.
Whoever wants to be first among you must be
your slave. That is what the Son of Man has done:
He came to serve, not to be served."*
MARK 10:43–45 MSG

We have an invisible person at our house named Not Me. Not Me is generous with her time and always offers quickly to help with chores and cleanup. Almost every time I ask for assistance, Not Me volunteers.

Sadly, many of us are quick to shove Not Me front and center when something needs to be done. But Jesus modeled a different philosophy. He came to serve.

Really, Lord? But I want to enjoy life too. Where's the fun in constantly putting someone else ahead of me?

When we use our gifts to bless others, He mysteriously heaps an even greater measure of rewards back on us. By giving away, you've multiplied your assets—you're now living in abundant joy, amazing peace, and astounding love. You're stockpiling heavenly riches!

Lord, show me how to live generously in service and love. Amen.

Day 107

GOD REWARDS
YOUR PATIENCE

To You I lift up my eyes, O You who are enthroned in the heavens! Behold, as the eyes of servants look to the hand of their master, as the eyes of a maid to the hand of her mistress, so our eyes look to the LORD our God, until He is gracious to us.
PSALM 123:1–2 NASB

You've prayed and prayed, and still God hasn't answered your plea for help and kindness. But, in reality, He *has*! He's behind the scenes, working things out on your behalf, setting the stage, getting all ready and into place.

Be assured God has a better plan than you could ever imagine. Your job is to keep looking to Him, knowing you'll see His answer.

Continue looking to God, your Lord and Master. He is and will forever be gracious. Keep your faith and your focus on Him, knowing that with Him all will turn out well.

Thank You, Lord, for Your love, grace, and kindness.
Build up my patience and peace as I keep my eyes on You.

TENDERLY LED

"I will win her back once again. I will lead her into the desert and speak tenderly to her there. I will return her vineyards to her and transform the Valley of Trouble into a gateway of hope. She will give herself to me there, as she did long ago when she was young."
HOSEA 2:14–15 NLT

Life may not be cradling you with gentle hands. You may feel battered by hardship and pain. But Jesus longs to speak tender words to your struggling soul. Whether you've been abandoned or abused or suffered from physical or emotional pain, He can transform your trouble into a place of hope. Give yourself to Him. Right in the midst of your hardship, step through His door of hope into freedom. The freedom of acceptance. The liberty of forgiveness. Dear friend, His purpose in your pain could be the redemption of your eternal soul.

Jesus, You don't desire hardship for me, but You can gently redeem it for Your purpose. Amen.

GOD'S POWER HEALS YOU

*Immediately her flow of blood was dried up at the source,
and [suddenly] she felt in her body that she was healed. . . .
And Jesus, recognizing in Himself that the power proceeding
from Him had gone forth, turned around immediately
in the crowd and said, Who touched My clothes?*
MARK 5:29–30 AMPC

A woman who'd been hemorrhaging for twelve years had spent all her money on doctors but was still not healed. She heard about Jesus, so she came up to Him amid the crowd and touched His garment. And immediately, Jesus' power entered her body and she was healed!

When she admitted to Jesus that it was she who'd touched Him, He said, "Daughter, your faith (your trust and confidence in Me, springing from faith in God) has restored you to health" (Mark 5:34 AMPC).

God has the power to heal. Yet you must have faith in that power when you reach out to Him.

*I believe You can heal me, Lord. You can restore me
physically, mentally, and spiritually. So I reach out
for You in this moment, awaiting Your power.*

Day 110
FORTRESS

How long will you assault me? Would all of you throw me
down—this leaning wall, this tottering fence? Surely they intend
to topple me from my lofty place; they take delight in lies. With
their mouths they bless, but in their hearts they curse. Yes, my
soul, find rest in God; my hope comes from him. Truly he is my
rock and my salvation; he is my fortress, I will not be shaken.
Psalm 62:3–6 niv

Do you ever feel as though you're surrounded by "frenemies"?
They say pretty words to your face, but inside they're secretly
hoping you tuck your dress into your underwear and parade
around the party with your fanny hanging out in the breeze.

Navigating this world is exhausting, but your vulnerable
spirit can find a safe place in Jesus. When the enemy assaults
you with vicious accusations, looking for weaknesses to exploit,
remember that you have a fortress.

Lord, remind me of Your truth in the face
of hurtful lies. In Jesus' name, amen.

Day 111

GOD QUIETS YOUR HEART

*Let be and be still, and know (recognize
and understand) that I am God.*
PSALM 46:10 AMPC

God wants you to be still. To obtain that quietness of heart, mind, soul, spirit, and body, you must believe that God is your "Refuge and Strength" (Psalm 46:1 AMPC). He has proven His help in times of trouble. So you need not fear, "though the earth should change and though the mountains be shaken into the midst of the seas, though its waters roar and foam, though the mountains tremble at its swelling and tumult" (Psalm 46:2–3 AMPC). God is your "High Tower" (Psalm 46:7 AMPC), the place you can go to rise above all fears and anxieties and simply rest in the one who holds the whole world in His hands.

*Lord, I come to You, relaxed in body. With You in my life,
I know I am safe, secure, and dearly loved. You alone help
me to rise above the fray and find a peace like no other.*

Day 112
HE SAID YES!

Whatever God has promised gets stamped with the Yes of Jesus. In Him, this is what we preach and pray, the great Amen, God's Yes and our Yes together, gloriously evident. God affirms us, making us a sure thing in Christ, putting his Yes within us. By his Spirit he has stamped us with his eternal pledge—a sure beginning of what he is destined to complete.
2 Corinthians 1:20–22 msg

We hear the disappointing denial of the word *no* all the time, especially if you have young children; your dialogue seems stuck on this dissatisfying response.

But no matter how many promises God has made to you, they are all "Yes!" in Jesus. He has filled you with the Holy Spirit and placed His stamp of ownership on your soul. Yes, you have been made new by the power of His blood. Yes, you can live in abundant joy. Yes, you are His cherished daughter. Yes, you have His supernatural power to resist sin. Yes, everlasting life in the glorious presence of God is yours! Nothing He has spoken to you will go unfulfilled.

Thank You, God, for Your yes. In the name of Jesus, amen!

GOD LEADS YOU
TO TRIUMPH

The wall was finished. . . . It had taken fifty-two days.
When all our enemies heard the news and all the
surrounding nations saw it, our enemies totally lost their
nerve. They knew that God was behind this work.
NEHEMIAH 6:15–16 MSG

Nehemiah had come up against a lot of challenges when he and the once-exiled Jews were building the wall around Jerusalem. Enemy leaders plotted to harm Nehemiah. Five times they sent him a message, trying to intimidate him, to discourage the workers, to undermine their determination. But instead of giving in to discouragement or fear, Nehemiah prayed to God, And the wall was completed in fifty-two days because God was behind all the efforts of His people!

God is behind all your efforts as well. No matter how many people plot to discourage you, pray to God for strength. Don't let any setbacks, obstacles, or disappointments keep you from doing what God has called you to do.

Thank You, Lord, for Your words of encouragement and
Your strength to complete all You have set my hands to do!

Day 114
FAITH OVER FEAR

"To whom will you compare me? Or who is my equal?"
says the Holy One. Lift up your eyes and look to the heavens:
Who created all these? He who brings out the starry host one
by one and calls forth each of them by name. Because of his
great power and mighty strength, not one of them is missing.
ISAIAH 40:25–26 NIV

What worries visit your mind at night when the world sleeps?
Your life is clutched in the grasp of the Holy One—the living
and powerful God of heaven and earth. Yield your life today to
the movements of His will. Don't allow the enemy to lie to you.
God is not ineffective or insufficient. He is lacking in no way.
There is no equal to His greatness!

Father, You are greater than my problems. You are the one
who holds everything together. Help me to trust. Amen.

Day 115

THE JOY OF GOD IS YOUR STRENGTH

Then [Ezra] told them, Go your way, eat the fat, drink the sweet
drink, and send portions to him for whom nothing is prepared;
for this day is holy to our Lord. And be not grieved and depressed,
for the joy of the Lord is your strength and stronghold.
NEHEMIAH 8:10 AMPC

After Jerusalem's wall was completed, Ezra read to the Jews the
book of the law of Moses. When the people had realized how
much they had strayed from God, they began to weep and moan.
But Ezra told them to not be depressed but to be full of joy because the joy of the Lord—their God who was full of forgiveness,
compassion, and grace; slow to anger; abounding in love (see
Nehemiah 9:17)—was their strength! He was their stronghold!

When you have joy in God and all He's done for you, you will
have the strength and be fortified, energized, and enabled to do
what He's already equipped you to do!

Lord, help me find the path to joy my relationship
with You provides. Overflow me with Your love and
forgiveness, Your strength and encouragement. In You
I find all the joy I could ever desire—and more!

Day 116
SOUL FOOD

"I am the bread of life. Your fathers ate the manna in the wilderness, and they died. This is the bread that comes down from heaven, so that one may eat of it and not die. I am the living bread that came down from heaven. If anyone eats of this bread, he will live forever. And the bread that I will give for the life of the world is my flesh."
JOHN 6:48–51 ESV

We indulge our appetites, but in a matter of hours we're feeling hunger pangs and craving something more. Our souls cry out to be filled as well. We partake of the world's buffet—money, perfectly toned abs, accolades, or acceptance—but its only temporary satisfaction. Soon we're empty again.

There is only one spiritual superfood capable of filling your void—the Bread of Life. What would happen if today you abandoned all your to-die-for substitutes for Him—the one who died for you?

Jesus, in You I have found what my soul craves. Amen.

Day 117

GOD COMMANDS YOU
TO KEEP FAITH

*Overhearing but ignoring what they said, Jesus said to
the ruler of the synagogue, Do not be seized with alarm
and struck with fear; only keep on believing.*
MARK 5:36 AMPC

Jairus, a leader of a synagogue, fell at Jesus' feet and begged Jesus to come lay His hands on his daughter, who was near death. Meanwhile, some people came and told Jairus that his daughter had died and asked why he continued to bother Jesus.

Jesus told Jairus, "Do not be seized with alarm and struck with fear; only keep on believing."

When Jesus arrived at Jairus' house, He told the grieving people that Jairus' daughter was just sleeping. After they laughed at Him, Jesus sent them out, and then He took the child's hand and told her to get up—and she did!

When your faith prompts you to go to Jesus, don't be discouraged by mockers, laughers, or discouragers. Follow Jesus' command: stay calm and keep believing. Jesus will work a miracle for you!

You do the impossible, Lord. In You I believe!

HE KNOWS NO LIMIT

*The earth is the Lord's and the fullness thereof, the world
and those who dwell therein, for he has founded it upon the
seas and established it upon the rivers. Who shall ascend the
hill of the Lord? And who shall stand in his holy place?*
PSALM 24:1–3 ESV

We have boundaries. These limits that our heavenly Father has
set on our lives are for our own good. But our smallness allows
us to appreciate His limitlessness. His presence stretches out
around us far beyond the ocean's borders. His power exceeds
the thundering strength of the most intimidating waves. He
created it all. And He is the God of it all. And He is the God of
me. And you.

When you reach the limit of your own strength, you will
find Him there. At the end of yourself, He waits to unveil to you
the immeasurable expanse of His great love, power, and grace.

*Lord, in my weakness You are strong. At the end of
my strength is Your unfathomable power. Amen.*

Day 119

GOD POURS ABUNDANT BLESSINGS UPON YOU

*And God is able to bless you abundantly, so that in
all things at all times, having all that you need,
you will abound in every good work.*
2 Corinthians 9:8 niv

As you continue to give of yourself and your resources to help
others and to serve God, He will continue to make sure you have
more than you need! Once you grasp this concept and test it, you'll
realize its truth. You'll become the eager, generous, and joyful
giver God created you to be.

Today, pray to God. Then have a "heart" talk with yourself,
deciding what you want to give—not just in terms of your money
but your talents, resources, and time. Fix it firm in your mind
that God will resupply whatever you expend. Then you will
become a lovely conduit through whom His heavenly blessings
will flow out onto the earth.

*Make me Your conduit of blessings, Lord!
Show me what I am to do. I'm ready to give!*

Day 120
COME

"Lord, if it's you," Peter replied, "tell me to come to you on the water." "Come," he said. Then Peter got down out of the boat, walked on the water and came toward Jesus.
MATTHEW 14:28–29 NIV

Are you the adventurous type? Or more likely to hang back, calculating the risk assessment? We tend to be a little hard on the apostle Peter for taking his eyes off Jesus and sinking into the waves. Yet we overlook the fact that Peter is the only one who got out of the boat! And because he did, he walked on the water with Jesus!

Jesus invites you too. Come into a deeper relationship with Him. Come and experience the awe of watching God work out His plan. Come and discover the unique purpose He has for your life. Are you willing to take a risk for Him today? Step out of the boat. See what God will do.

Lord, give me courage to step into
Your purpose for my life. Amen.

GOD HELPS YOU OVERCOME THE DOUBT IN YOUR HEART

*Jesus said, "If? There are no 'ifs' among believers.
Anything can happen." . . . The father cried,
"Then I believe. Help me with my doubts!"*
MARK 9:23–24 MSG

A man came to Jesus with his son who had fits that exposed him to danger. The disciples had been unable to help. So the father said to Jesus, "If you can do anything, do it. Have a heart and help us!" (Mark 9:22 MSG). Jesus replied, "If? There are no 'ifs' among believers. Anything can happen." And the man replied, "Then I believe. Help me with my doubts!" Within minutes, Jesus rid the boy of the spirit and helped him stand.

You may have had occasions when you wondered if Jesus could do the impossible. When that happens, go to Jesus. Even if you don't see any way forward, He does!

I believe, Lord. Help me with my unbelief!

REMEMBER

*"Remember the things I have done in the past. For I
alone am God! I am God, and there is none like me.
Only I can tell you the future before it even happens.
Everything I plan will come to pass."*
ISAIAH 46:9–10 NLT

Remembering. We cherish our memories of good times and even
hard times that strengthened us. It's important not to forget
where you've come from because your past has chiseled you into
the unique person you are.

God says, "Remember the things I have done in the past."
If you find yourself doubting God's goodness, His ability to
straighten out the kinks in your day, His love for you, or His
power, just look back. You'll see the evidence of His guiding
presence and find fresh faith!

*Heavenly Father, bring Your past deliverances and
mercies to mind when doubt assaults me. Amen.*

GOD WORKS ALL THINGS FOR GOOD

*We know that God causes everything to work
together for the good of those who love God
and are called according to his purpose for them.*
ROMANS 8:28 NLT

Sometimes bad things happen to good people. Consider Lazarus. When Lazarus was ill, the sisters sent word to Jesus. But Jesus stayed where He was for two more days before He began making His way to Bethany. By the time He arrived, Lazarus had been dead four days.

On His way to Lazarus' resting place, Jesus wept. On His arrival, He yelled, "Lazarus, come out!" (John 11:43 NLT), and he did. And all who believed saw God's glory!

God has called you for a purpose. He has a plan for your life. Although you may not understand on this side of heaven why something has happened, you can be assured God is working things together for your good. Believe in Him, trust in His ways, and you too will see God's glory.

*Lord, I know You have a plan to work all things
for good. Help me to trust in this truth.*

Day 124
MISFIT

Then the word of the Lord came to him: "This man will not be your heir, but a son who is your own flesh and blood will be your heir." He took him outside and said, "Look up at the sky and count the stars—if indeed you can count them." Then he said to him, "So shall your offspring be." Abram believed the Lord, and he credited it to him as righteousness.
GENESIS 15:4–6 NIV

Have you ever felt inadequate in your faith? This feeling can creep into your thought life, especially after a bout of human stumbling. But don't let your stumble define you. God is in the business of using misfits like. . .

Abraham, who lied and didn't exactly trust God to handle things, yet he fathered a nation and was considered righteous.

Moses, who was a murderer and had a hot temper, yet he led a nation out of slavery and through a sea.

David, who was an adulterer, a murderer, and not exactly the father of the year, yet he was a man after God's own heart and a great king of Israel.

We've all sinned, but God can still transform you into a woman of virtue. Trust His promises.

Father, I choose to trust You. Amen.

GOD RE-CREATED YOU FOR GOOD WORKS

We are God's [own] handiwork (His workmanship), recreated in Christ Jesus, [born anew] that we may do those good works which God predestined (planned beforehand) for us [taking paths which He prepared ahead of time], that we should walk in them [living the good life which He prearranged and made ready for us to live].
EPHESIANS 2:10 AMPC

God has had you in and on His mind since before the world or you were created. He's already figured out what paths you are to take, and He's prepared your way down them. He's prearranged everything so you can live the purpose for which He created you!

You have a purpose in this world. And if you're ever unclear about what that purpose is, go to God and ask Him to lay it out. Be reassured when things don't turn out like you thought they would, knowing that whatever happens, all will be well. God is with you, going before you, and protecting you from behind.

Thank You for having a plan, Lord. Show me where You'd have me walk, what You'd have me do!

Day 126

A PLACE TO BELONG

"My Father's house has many rooms; if that were not so,
would I have told you that I am going there to prepare a place
for you? And if I go and prepare a place for you, I will come
back and take you to be with me that you also may be where
I am. You know the way to the place where I am going."
JOHN 14:2–4 NIV

This world is more like a hallway or merely a front porch to heaven—it sure doesn't seem to provide much protection from foul weather. Friend, there's a better place waiting for us. And God is pulling out all the stops! Imagine a home where the stain of sin is wiped away—perfect immortal bodies, free from pain and illness; people who delight in righteousness, who have no anger, jealousy, or hatred, or steal; a landscape more beautiful than a finely manicured park, with no dead leaves or decayed wood; and the ultimate experience of living in God's glorious presence, day after day after day!

Jesus, thank You for the hope of my forever home. Amen.

Day 127

GOD REWARDS YOUR PERSEVERANCE

*Now He was telling them a parable to show that at all
times they ought to pray and not to lose heart.*
LUKE 18:1 NASB

Jesus told the disciples a parable. . . . It seems a widow kept
coming to a judge, telling him her rights were being violated
and demanding protection from those against her. But the judge
ignored her time and time again. Finally, he said to himself,
"Even though I do not fear God nor respect man, yet because
this widow bothers me, I will give her legal protection" (Luke
18:4–5 NASB).

When you are looking for God to right a wrong, to step into
your situation, don't stop with one prayer. Continue to cry out
to Him, knowing that He, in His compassion, is already working behind the scenes to bring you justice, responding to your
pleas. Do not lose heart!

*God, here is my plea: In Your compassion, respond
to my prayer. I will not lose heart but will trust You
are setting things right for me—to Your glory!*

YOUR TRUE LIFE

"Therefore I tell you, do not worry about your life, what you will eat or drink; or about your body, what you will wear. Is not life more than food, and the body more than clothes? Look at the birds of the air; they do not sow or reap or store away in barns, and yet your heavenly Father feeds them. Are you not much more valuable than they? Can any one of you by worrying add a single hour to your life?"
MATTHEW 6:25–27 NIV

Your heavenly Father wants you to grasp His hand in total trust, fully expecting that He is able to provide for your needs, to bring plentiful goodness and abundant joy into your day-to-day journey despite its trials. He wants you to live with an attitude of peace, far from the nasty lies of the enemy. Trust Him with your troubles and receive victory and freedom to enjoy the colors of a butterfly's wing, to picnic in the sun while your children giggle and dance in the wildflowers, and to lighten someone's burden with a helping hand.

Father, may I trust You so fully that I can live the abundant life You intended. In Jesus' name, amen.

GOD REWARDS YOUR COMMITMENT TO HIM

*"Remember what happened to Lot's wife! If you grasp
and cling to life on your terms, you'll lose it, but if you
let that life go, you'll get life on God's terms."*
LUKE 17:32–33 MSG

Abraham's cousin Lot was living in the sinful city of Sodom, which God was about to destroy. At Abraham's request, God sent two angels to drag Lot and his family out of town before its destruction. One of the angels told them, "Don't look back or stop anywhere in the valley!" (Genesis 19:17 NLT). But Lot's wife "looked back as she was following behind him, and she turned into a pillar of salt" (Genesis 19:26 NLT).

Jesus wants you to learn from Lot's wife. He asks that you not cling to a life lived on your terms but to live your life on God's terms. When you do, you'll gain true life, and He'll reward your commitment to Him!

*Help me, Lord, to be more focused on You than
anything else. I want to live my life on Your terms
because I know that's the best choice I could ever make.*

Day 130

FOR HIS GLORY

"The servant given one thousand said, 'Master, I know you have high standards and hate careless ways, that you demand the best and make no allowances for error. I was afraid I might disappoint you, so I found a good hiding place and secured your money. Here it is, safe and sound down to the last cent.' The master was furious. 'That's a terrible way to live! It's criminal to live cautiously like that! If you knew I was after the best, why did you do less than the least? The least you could have done would have been to invest the sum with the bankers, where at least I would have gotten a little interest. Take the thousand and give it to the one who risked the most. And get rid of this "play-it-safe" who won't go out on a limb. Throw him out into utter darkness.' "
MATTHEW 25:24–30 MSG

What thing in your life makes your heart skip in anticipation? Have you ever considered that God planted that desire, that special talent, in your makeup for His glory? Your actions here on earth do matter. God is whispering to you today, "That thing you love to do—I gave it to you for a reason—come and do it for Me!"

God, I give You my talents. Use them for Your purpose. Amen.

GOD GIVES YOU DIRECT ACCESS TO HIM

For it is through Him that we both [whether far off or near]
now have an introduction (access) by one [Holy] Spirit
to the Father [so that we are able to approach Him].
EPHESIANS 2:18 AMPC

Adam and Eve desired to go their own way, and sin entered the world, separating the holy from the unholy.

Then God sent Jesus. The reconciler. The one who ended the hostility, eliminated the conflict. The one who has saved those willing to believe. Once again, you can approach the one who calls you His beloved. You have access to the Creator of the world through the Holy Spirit, who presents you before the throne of God.

God loved you so much that He allowed His only Son to die on the cross. He bridged the gap for you and for me. Draw near to God—and He will be sure to draw near to you (see James 4:8).

I thank You, God, with all my heart for all You
have done, all You have allowed to be sacrificed
just so I could be close to You once more.

Day 132
WALK BY FAITH

So we are always of good courage. We know that while we are at home in the body we are away from the Lord, for we walk by faith, not by sight. Yes, we are of good courage, and we would rather be away from the body and at home with the Lord. So whether we are at home or away, we make it our aim to please him.
2 Corinthians 5:6–9 esv

The world says that faith is blind. But our faith recognizes that this world isn't all there is to life. It's our trust in what we hope for—the things we know are waiting for us in eternity—that keeps us going and gives our faith something to grab on to in the hard times.

But how do we know a fabulous eternal life awaits? The "eyes" of your faith can see the truth, and your long, intimate journey with God provides the evidence. Make it your goal to please Him, to look for His movement around you, and to find out all you can about the Creator who loves you. Then your absolute certainty of the truth of all His promises will deepen.

God, open my eyes of faith. I want to step out confidently, knowing every word You've spoken is concrete truth. Amen.

Day 133

GOD REJOICES OVER YOU

The Lord your God is in the midst of you, a Mighty One, a Savior
[Who saves]! He will rejoice over you with joy; He will rest [in silent
satisfaction] and in His love He will be silent and make no mention
[of past sins, or even recall them]; He will exult over you with singing.
ZEPHANIAH 3:17 AMPC

When you seek God with all your being and follow His ways, He's delighted! As you rejoice in Him and trust Him, He's so happy He sings over you! Because Jesus died for your sins, God makes no mention of your missteps and mistakes. As a believer, your sins have been removed from you "as far as the east is from the west" (Psalm 103:12 NASB).

Today consider what God has done for you. Plant in your mind a picture of Him rejoicing over you, pouring out His love, singing over you. Then sing your song of praise—the one He's planted in your heart—to Him. Revel and rejoice together as one!

Lord, You've done so much for me! I'm overwhelmed by Your song.
May I praise You with the new song You've planted within me!

SHOW YOUR LOVE

The third time he said to him, "Simon son of John, do you love me?" Peter was hurt because Jesus asked him the third time, "Do you love me?" He said, "Lord, you know all things; you know that I love you." Jesus said, "Feed my sheep."
JOHN 21:17 NIV

God loves all His children with a depth of affection unfathomable to our limited minds. And He doesn't just say the words; He proves them in action. God loves you so much that He sent His beloved Son to die for you to heal the rift between you.

Following Jesus isn't an empty religion of rituals; it's a deep, abiding relationship with the God who loves you. Jesus told Peter if he loved Him to feed His sheep. He longs for you to return His love as well. But He wants more than empty words.

Show Him your love today through your actions.

*Father, Your love is total and full, beautiful
and amazing. I love You too. Amen.*

GOD CALLS INTO BEING THINGS THAT WERE NOT

He is our father in the sight of God, in whom he believed—
the God who gives life to the dead and calls into being
things that were not. Against all hope, Abraham in hope
believed and so became the father of many nations, just as
it had been said to him, "So shall your offspring be."
ROMANS 4:17–18 NIV

Imagine being Abraham. God told him he'd be the father of many nations. Yet year after year went by without a son in sight. But Abraham knew his God. He hoped against all hope that he would be given a son, which finally happened when Abraham was one hundred years old and his wife Sarah, ninety! Why did Abraham believe? Because God had said so!

God can do anything at any time anywhere. Believe in that power, that your loving God can call anything into being. Never lose hope. God *will* come through for you. There is no limit to what He can do to fulfill His desire and meet yours.

God, I know there's no limit to what You can do.
You alone can work miracles in my life!

A BIT OF KINDNESS

*Put on then, as God's chosen ones, holy and beloved, compassionate
hearts, kindness, humility, meekness, and patience, bearing with
one another and, if one has a complaint against another, forgiving
each other; as the Lord has forgiven you, so you also must forgive.*
Colossians 3:12–13 esv

Kindness might seem like a small thing to you—holding a door
for a loaded-down mom, raking your elderly neighbor's leaves,
smiling at that grumpy coworker—but kindness expands just
like the ripples on a pond. Each kind act touches the life of
someone beside you and brings hope and a spark of brightness
to their spirit.

God's kindness to us is also attractive. His grace draws us in
to hear His truth. Your kindness can also draw others to Jesus.
In a world fueled by self-focus and me-me-me attitudes, anyone who sees your kindness will wonder why you'd bother. You
never know what far-reaching results a little drop of kindness
might have.

*God, show me where a bit of kindness could
spread Your love around me. Amen.*

GOD KEEPS HIS PROMISES

No unbelief or distrust made him waver (doubtingly question)
concerning the promise of God, but he grew strong and was
empowered by faith as he gave praise and glory to God,
fully satisfied and assured that God was able and mighty
to keep His word and to do what He had promised.
ROMANS 4:20–21 AMPC

Can you imagine trusting so much in God's promises that, as the years of waiting go by, you grow stronger and more empowered by your faith? Can you imagine praising God for a promise not yet delivered?

That's what Abraham did! And there's more! Because of his amazing faith, God "credited to him" as righteousness (right standing with God) (Romans 4:23 AMPC). These words and this story were not just recorded for Abraham's benefit, but for yours!

What promise are you counting on God fulfilling? Follow Abraham's example, and praise God for already bringing it to pass—even if you're still waiting. As you do, you will grow strong, and your faith will empower you!

> *God, I'm waiting on this promise. . . .*
> *And I praise You for bringing it to pass!*

NEVER BEYOND HIS REACH

God raised us up with Christ and seated us with him in the
heavenly realms in Christ Jesus, in order that in the coming ages
he might show the incomparable riches of his grace, expressed
in his kindness to us in Christ Jesus. For it is by grace you have
been saved, through faith—and this is not from yourselves,
it is the gift of God—not by works, so that no one can boast.
EPHESIANS 2:6–9 NIV

Do you have secrets? Maybe you've said terrible words, maybe you've done horrible things, or maybe you've felt shameful emotions. Whatever the case, there's hope.

You can never outrun God's mercy or cross the borders of His grace. No matter what you've done or what's been done to you, you're never beyond His reach. God can lift your face and wash away your stains in the crimson flood of Jesus' blood. He can clothe you in mercy and seat you with Jesus at His table in heaven. Bring your secrets to the light of His forgiveness, and bask in the glow of His extravagant grace.

Jesus, my shame is gone! My fear is gone! I never imagined I could
feel clean again. But You washed it all away. Thank You. Amen.

GOD GIVES YOU REST

Come to Me, all you who labor and are heavy-laden
and overburdened, and I will cause you to rest.
[I will ease and relieve and refresh your souls.]
MATTHEW 11:28 AMPC

You can relax, be yourself, be calm, and be renewed when you're with someone who has the best in mind for you. Who will do anything for you. Who loves you just as you love him or her.

Jesus is that person. You can trust Him with your heart, soul, spirit, troubles, and your very life, for He is the one who gave up His life blood for you so you could be reconciled to God. When you are in Jesus' presence, the one who calls you friend, you can tell Him everything that's going on—your problems, your hopes, your dreams. Or you can sit in companionable silence, just soaking in His love. And He's the one who will never leave or forsake you.

> *Beloved Jesus, I come to You today knowing*
> *You're waiting to relieve and refresh me.*

YOU CAN FIND HIM

"Starting from scratch, he made the entire human race and made the earth hospitable, with plenty of time and space for living so we could seek after God, and not just grope around in the dark but actually find him. He doesn't play hide-and-seek with us. He's not remote; he's near. We live and move in him, can't get away from him!"
ACTS 17:26–28 MSG

At times we look around for God and can't seem to see Him, but God isn't playing games with you. He wants to be found and known and loved by you. He wants a deep and meaningful relationship with you, His beloved daughter. God doesn't delight in confusion and tricks, and He won't hold Himself back from you if you search for Him. He's near. Ask God to step into the light. And He will show Himself to you.

God, thank You for being closer to me than
I imagined. Walk with me today. Amen.

Day 141

GOD IS MOVED BY
YOUR PRAYERS

After that God was moved by prayer.
2 Samuel 21:14 nasb

Jesus said, "When you pray, go into your [most] private room, and, closing the door, pray to your Father, Who is in secret; and your Father, Who sees in secret, will reward you in the open" (Matthew 6:6 AMPC). But how do you know God has heard you? The Bible says that you can be confident that when you ask anything according to His will, God hears you. And because you know He hears you, you know you'll receive what you have asked (see 1 John 5:14–15).

God is moved by your prayers. Plant that knowledge, that fact, that truth deep within your inner being. And your mustard-seed faith will grow beyond what you could ever hope or imagine.

My beloved Father God, I come to You in secret,
to have a heart-to-heart talk with You,
knowing You hear me and will answer.

Day 142
YOU ARE ACCEPTED

"Those the Father has given me will come to me, and I will never reject them. For I have come down from heaven to do the will of God who sent me, not to do my own will. And this is the will of God, that I should not lose even one of all those he has given me, but that I should raise them up at the last day."

JOHN 6:37–39 NLT

Isn't it a relief that we don't have to clean ourselves up for God? He's already familiar with all our ugly messes anyway. We're free to bring every problem to Him. Don't listen to Satan's lies. You haven't done anything God hasn't seen before. You can't shock Him with your sin. Instead, He says, "Come"—without fear of rejection, without punishment and shame. There's a place for you at God's banquet. Pull up a chair and take your place. Daughter of the King, His grace covers all.

Lord, I haven't been honest with You. I've tried to hide my problems. But I'm coming to You now. Forgive me. Amen.

GOD DELIGHTS IN MY HUMBLE FAITH

For the Lord takes delight in his people;
he crowns the humble with victory.
PSALM 149:4 NIV

Jeremiah prayed, "Lord God! Behold, You have made the heavens and the earth by Your great power and by Your outstretched arm! There is nothing too hard or too wonderful for You" (Jeremiah 32:17 AMPC). He goes on to say God has His eyes open to people's ways and rewards them accordingly (see Jeremiah 32:19).

When you have a problem and see no solution, when you're trapped in a situation and see no way out, cry out to God with all your heart. Be humble, telling Him, "Lord, we both know I can't do this—but I believe You can!" And He'll meet you in the midst of it all, rewarding you with peace and victory!

Lord, You know what I'm up against. You know I
can't do this—but You can! So I'm leaving this in
Your hands because nothing is too hard for You.

Day 144

FINGERPRINTS OF
THE CREATOR

*For ever since the world was created, people have seen the
earth and sky. Through everything God made, they can
clearly see his invisible qualities—his eternal power and divine
nature. So they have no excuse for not knowing God.*

ROMANS 1:20 NLT

God has not left us without evidence of Himself. In fact,
He planted us firmly in a world teeming with proof of His existence. It stretches above you in a clear night sky sprinkled with
sparkling stars. It's in the burning light of dawn that unfurls
from the horizon. It's in the dewdrops that cling to spring tulips
and the crickets' song that follows a sweltering summer afternoon.
You can find it in the blazing fall colors and the stark winter snow.

Open your eyes and see the signs. Walk through His creation
today. Search for His fingerprints of love, and you will find Him
there.

Father, open my eyes to all Your invisible qualities. Amen.

GOD WANTS YOUR ALL

*Jesus said to him, "No one, after putting his hand to the
plow and looking back, is fit for the kingdom of God."*
LUKE 9:62 NASB

To be fit for the kingdom of God, you need to be totally committed, not looking back. Like a farmer, if your hand is on the plow
but your eyes are focused on what's behind you, you'll quickly
veer off course and create crooked furrows.

The apostle Paul aspired to "forgetting what lies behind and
straining forward to what lies ahead" (Philippians 3:13 AMPC).
He pressed "on toward the goal to win the prize for which God
has called me heavenward in Christ Jesus" (Philippians 3:14 NIV).

God wants your all—for His sake and your own. So keep
looking forward, and you'll see the clear path to God's kingdom!

*Lord, help me not be swayed into looking back to
the world but forward to the prospect of heaven!*

PERFECT PEACE

"Peace I leave with you; my peace I give to you.
Not as the world gives do I give to you. Let not your
hearts be troubled, neither let them be afraid."
JOHN 14:27 ESV

Is anyone completely selfless and good? Only God! This world's hidden strings aren't attached to His gifts. The peace He offers is legitimate and guaranteed for all eternity. It won't wheeze its dying breath two hours after the warranty expires. His unlimited coverage permeates every facet of your life.

Is worry leaving you exhausted? His peace covers that. Are busy schedules leaving you frantic? His peace covers that too. Is fear over the future robbing your joy? Yep, His peace has you covered.

His gifts are not an illusion. You can live enveloped in His peace when you hold firmly to His grasp and surrender to His will. Trust Him today.

Jesus, thank You that You don't offer false promises.
I can trust You to keep me in perfect peace. Amen.

GOD SHOWERS YOU
WITH BLESSINGS

[My people] shall dwell safely. . .and sleep [confidently]. . . .
And I will make them and the places round about My hill a blessing,
and I will cause the showers to come down in their season; there
shall be showers of blessing [of good insured by God's favor].
EZEKIEL 34:25–26 AMPC

Because you are a believer in Jesus, there is peace between you
and God. You have been given His Holy Spirit. Jesus dwells within
you, and you now dwell in God. Because of this, you can walk
without fear. You can live safely and sleep peacefully. You are
filled with hope, courage, strength, and power to do what He's
called you to do. And best of all, you can wait for the never-ending
showers of blessings that God rains down on you.

Look around you today. Take note of all the blessings surrounding you. Dig into the Word, and ask God to reveal the good
message He has for you in this quiet moment.

You are so good to me, Lord. Thank You
so much for all You have blessed me with.

Day 148

YOU ARE REDEEMED

In their fright the women bowed down with their faces to the ground, but the men said to them, "Why do you look for the living among the dead? He is not here; he has risen! Remember how he told you, while he was still with you in Galilee."
LUKE 24:5–6 NIV

"Why do you look for the living among the dead?" the angel asked. The women were confused. They hadn't yet realized that the empty tomb symbolized the fullness of new life. And the dawning realization that Jesus was alive brought a flood of hope. Their despair changed to dancing. Light flooded into the darkness of this world. Their lives would never be the same again. An empty tomb proved Jesus could not be held by death's constraints. He lives!

Jesus changes lives yet today, and He can change yours too.

Lord, thank You for a redeemed life in You. Amen.

GOD TRANSFORMS YOUR PANIC TO PRAISE AND PEACE

O God, have mercy on me, for people are hounding me.
My foes attack me all day long. . . . But when I am afraid,
I will put my trust in you. I praise God for what he has
promised. I trust in God, so why should I be afraid?
PSALM 56:1, 3–4 NLT

Many things can induce panic: threats of war, shootings, ter-
rorist attacks, hurricanes, tornadoes, earthquakes, job loss,
health challenges, and so on. As a believer, you can rely on your
confidence in your mighty God. You can choose to trust Him,
knowing He's made certain promises to you. With God on your
side, there's nothing any human or circumstances can do to you.

When you place your confidence in God, you're making a
conscious decision to respond spiritually instead of reacting
emotionally. To get from panic to praise and peace, tell God
what's disturbing you. Tell Him you trust Him. Recall what
God has done in the past, and then praise Him for keeping His
promises, affirming His vow to guard you. And soon peace will
reign within.

Lord, here's what happening. . . . I trust You to see me
through, and I praise You for what You've promised.
Thank You for the peace that gives me.

Day 150

AGED TO PERFECTION

*"Stand up in the presence of the aged, show respect
for the elderly and revere your God. I am the Lord."*
LEVITICUS 19:32 NIV

Sometimes our attitude toward the elderly is misguided. Their exterior has lost the sparkle of newness and looks a bit worse for wear, so we assume they've lost their value. Some even think they've outlived their usefulness.

But God values the life of each and every person. Each one is precious to Him, created in His image with a specific purpose in mind. And you can't outlive God's purpose for your life. But our definition of useful and God's definition might not match up. Sit with them and soak in their wisdom. Hold their hand and listen. After all, their purpose could be to share with you the insight they've accumulated after decades of walking with Jesus.

*God, help me see the value of each person
through Your eyes. In Jesus' name, amen.*

GOD COLLECTS YOUR TEARS

*You keep track of all my sorrows. You have collected all
my tears in your bottle. You have recorded each one in
your book. . . . This I know: God is on my side!*

PSALM 56:8–9 NLT

It's comforting to know that God cares so deeply about you
that He weeps when you weep. That He's eager and willing to
heal and mend your broken heart, to bind up your wounds (see
Psalm 147:3).

So when the blues come calling, cry on God's shoulder.
Take heart that He knows what's happening and is on your
side. And all the while, take comfort as you remember that
one day your loving God "will wipe every tear" from your eyes,
"and there will be no more death or sorrow or crying or pain"
(Revelation 21:4 NLT).

*Thank You, Lord, for loving me so much that You collect my tears!
Mend my broken heart, and reassure me with Your warm embrace
of peace and hope. I rise with courage, knowing You're on my side!*

Day 152
IN CHARGE

Our God is in the heavens; he does all that he pleases.
PSALM 115:3 ESV

As grown-ups we often suffer from delusions of grandeur when it comes to our perceived control over our world. Sometimes a taste of power has us convinced we can plan our destiny without God. Other times we seem to be convinced that our worrying and anxiety will somehow prevent unwanted things from entering our universe.

Thankfully we belong to a God who is large and in charge. His plans will come to pass as He pleases. But we can rest in the knowledge that all our mistakes and power plays will never succeed in wrestling control from His grasp. So relax today in the knowledge that He loves you and that you belong to the powerful God of creation.

*Lord, I surrender to Your control. I belong
to You, who has the power. Amen.*

GOD HAS CHOSEN YOU, HOLY AND BELOVED

So, as those who have been chosen of God, holy and beloved,
put on a heart of compassion, kindness, humility, gentleness and
patience; bearing with one another, and forgiving each other. . .just
as the Lord forgave you. . . . Beyond all these things put on love.
COLOSSIANS 3:12–14 NASB

Because of Jesus' sacrifice and your acceptance of Him in your life, you are now accepted and holy in God's eyes. But when you began to believe, you did not automatically take on the Christ-like attributes of compassion, kindness, humility, gentleness, and patience. Yet you now have the responsibility to adopt them. At the same time, you are to forgive others just as God forgave you. And above all, put on love.

This may sound like a tall order. It's certainly one you cannot fulfill on your own. But there is no need to despair. Simply surrender yourself to the control of God's Spirit. He alone will bring you to the place God wants you to be!

Lord, I surrender myself to the control of Your Spirit. Help me to
be compassionate, kind, humble, gentle, patient, and forgiving.
Above all, help me give others the love You've given me!

Day 154
A CLEANER PURPOSE

Run from anything that stimulates youthful lusts. Instead,
pursue righteous living, faithfulness, love, and peace. Enjoy the
companionship of those who call on the Lord with pure hearts.
2 TIMOTHY 2:22 NLT

When we first come to Jesus, it can be difficult to give up the ways of this world. But as you begin to live on a diet of the Bread of Life, your tastes for the things of this world will sour. Keep turning to His Word when the hankering for old ways hits you, and soon you'll be craving the pure living habits of faithfulness, love, and obedience.

Father, give me strength to resist temptation.
You have a better purpose for me. Amen.

GOD PROTECTS AND PROSPERS YOU

Don't worry about the wicked or envy those who do wrong. For like grass, they soon fade away. Like spring flowers, they soon wither. Trust in the LORD and do good. Then you will live safely in the land and prosper.

PSALM 37:1–3 NLT

Even though it *looks* like the ungodly "have it all," God's Word says those who don't stand right with Him will be like grass and flowers, fading away and withering. Meanwhile, because you trust in the Lord and do good things, God promises you'll live safely and prosper!

Consider the demise of the cruel queen Jezebel, who seemed to have it all. After she fixed her hair and makeup, her eunuchs pushed her out a window. She was then trampled by horses and eaten by dogs. All that was left when they came to bury her was her skull, feet, and the palms of her hands.

Don't worry about the "haves." Instead, trust God. He'll give you true life!

I'm so glad I long for and trust in You more than wealth or power, Lord. With You, I know I'll find true safety and prosperity.

YOUR TRUE PURPOSE

*Do your best. Work from the heart for your real Master,
for God, confident that you'll get paid in full when you
come into your inheritance. Keep in mind always that
the ultimate Master you're serving is Christ.*
COLOSSIANS 3:23–24 MSG

A tower of dirty dishes glares at you over the rim of your sink.
You have a choice to make. And it involves your attitude. Ouch!
No one enjoys an attitude check. *Isn't it enough, Lord, that I just get
through my daily tasks? You mean I actually have to bring You glory out of
this pile of pans? Okay fine—one attitude adjustment coming up.*

As you plunk the first dish into the water, you thank God
for taking your dirty, sin-stained life and washing away all the
grime, for shining you up and showing you His purpose for your
days. . . . The next thing you know, you're singing praises to God
in your sparkling kitchen!

*God, my true purpose is to work for You
in whatever task is before me. Amen.*

GOD GIVES YOU YOUR HEART'S DESIRE

*Delight yourself also in the Lord, and He will give you the desires
and secret petitions of your heart. Commit your way to the Lord
[roll and repose each care of your load on Him]; trust (lean on,
rely on, and be confident) also in Him and He will bring it to pass.*
PSALM 37:4–5 AMPC

The more you keep company with God, the more you'll learn
to know Him and His will for your life. So take steps to delight
yourself in the Lord. Spend time reading His Word, sitting with
Him, handing Him all your troubles and challenges, and com-
mitting your feet to His path. As you do so, your heart's desires
will begin to line up with His. That's when God will make your
wishes become reality! Those heart's desires will not be the things
you want to accomplish apart from God but will be those things
that bring you true peace and satisfaction (see Psalm 37:37).

*Lord, I find such delight in You and Your ways!
Reveal my true heart's desire as I commit all
that I am to You. I trust You will bring it to pass!*

CORRAL YOUR THOUGHTS

*The weapons of our warfare are not of the flesh but have
divine power to destroy strongholds. We destroy arguments
and every lofty opinion raised against the knowledge of
God, and take every thought captive to obey Christ.*
2 CORINTHIANS 10:4–5 ESV

Our thoughts can wreak havoc on our lives when we allow them
to run loose. One concern enters our head and, if left unattended, can spill a whole can of worry worms. Before you can
say, "Scat, cat!" you're wringing your hands and headed for the
aspirin bottle.

But God doesn't intend for you to be ruled by random
thoughts. Even though it can seem as hopeless as herding cats,
corner those thoughts! Speak God's truth and demolish the
devil's lies.

*Heavenly Father, show me when my thoughts are
running wild and leading me into sin. Amen.*

GOD TURNS YOUR MOURNING INTO JOY

Weeping may stay for the night, but rejoicing comes in the morning. . . . You turned my wailing into dancing; you removed my sackcloth and clothed me with joy, that my heart may sing your praises and not be silent. LORD my God, I will praise you forever.
PSALM 30:5, 11–12 NIV

David had enemies after him, his health was threatened, his soul was in a dark place, and at some point, God seemed angry then distant (see Psalm 30:1–3, 5, 7). But David cried out to God and was lifted above enemies, healed, brought into the light, was again favored and helped by God. His wailing was turned into dancing. His mourning replaced with joy. David's heart couldn't help but sing God's praises.

When you're mourning a loss—whether it be that of a loved one, home, marriage, job, or some treasure—don't despair. Although you may do some weeping, have confidence that God will turn your mourning into joy.

Thank You, Lord, for always being there when I need You, for helping me to understand this mourning will one day pass, and for turning my darkness into light!

YOUR KINGDOM PURPOSE

*He has told you, O man, what is good; and what does
the LORD require of you but to do justice, and to love
kindness, and to walk humbly with your God?*
MICAH 6:8 ESV

Too often we're fatally nearsighted and hyper-focused on fin-
ishing whatever task has captured our attention, and we miss
the greater purpose God has given us. What kingdom work have
you overlooked because you're distracted? Are you loving the
ones in your care? Are you spreading kindness and teaching
your children how to walk with Jesus? Or are you distracted by
eternally inconsequential details?

Lord, may I not overlook my kingdom work today. Amen.

GOD GIFTS YOU WITH LOVE, GRACE, AND FAITH

*It is by grace you have been saved, through faith—
and this is not from yourselves, it is the gift of God—
not by works, so that no one can boast.*
EPHESIANS 2:8–9 NIV

The only reason God sent His Son Jesus into the world is because He loves you and wants to save you. The apostle John makes this clear when he writes, "God showed how much he loved us by sending his one and only Son into the world so that we might have eternal life through him. This is real love—not that we loved God, but that he loved us and sent his Son as a sacrifice to take away our sins" (1 John 4:9–10 NLT).

That means there is nothing you can ever do—no good works, money, or any other effort—to earn the gifts of saving grace and faith. It's a done deal!

*I am amazed, Lord, at what You have so freely given to
me—and all because You love me! I am so filled with joy
from that knowledge. Thank You, Father, for your precious
gifts of love, faith, and grace, which I can never repay.*

Day 162

STRAIGHT ON TO HEAVEN

And such were some of you. But you were washed,
you were sanctified, you were justified in the name of
the Lord Jesus Christ and by the Spirit of our God.
1 CORINTHIANS 6:11 ESV

Have you ever become overconfident, taken your eyes off Jesus for a moment, and found yourself back in the same place where you started? Peter experienced a little of that as he looked away from Jesus during his stroll on the sea. He sank. And you will too. Thankfully Jesus was there to pull him out.

This world can be pretty persuasive: "No one will notice if you skip a Sunday now and then to sleep in." "It's okay if you pass on that bit of news you heard about your friend."

Be careful, dear one. Without the guiding truth of scripture, you could end up circling right back to sins that held you captive in the past.

Heavenly Father, the words "such were some of you"
are so sweet. Guide me straight on till heaven. Amen.

Day 163

GOD LEADS YOU
BY THE HAND

Your path led through the sea, your way through the mighty
waters, though your footprints were not seen. You led your
people like a flock by the hand of Moses and Aaron.
PSALM 77:19–20 NIV

Many Old Testament stories of endurance, challenges, and dangers were recorded so that God's people might learn from them and take from them encouragement and hope (see Romans 15:4). From the story of the Red Sea crossing (see Exodus 14) and today's verses from the psalms, it's clear that at times God may lead you through places that seem a little scary and down pathways you would never have thought open. Like the Israelites, although you may not see God's footprints on the path before you, you can be sure God is leading you through the mighty waters, that His presence is very real.

Although I cannot see Your face or footprints, I know
You are with me. Lead me where You would have me
go, and I will walk willingly. My trust is in You.

Day 164
COURAGE TO BE REAL

So speak encouraging words to one another.
Build up hope so you'll all be together in this,
no one left out, no one left behind.
1 THESSALONIANS 5:11 MSG

Social media is great for staying connected, but it's also far too easy to edit your life right out of reality and into your perfect version of yourself. Have you ever cropped out the mess along the edge of your picture?

Sweet, struggling sister, Jesus never called anyone to be perfect—He called you to persevere despite your missteps. Ain't nobody perfect—only Jesus! We've all sinned and fallen short of the glory of God—that's hardly a shocker to anyone with a Bible. And if you pretend to have it all together, you may miss God's purpose for your trials. When you come through tough waters, you can turn around and help those struggling behind you.

Lord, give me courage to be real in my faith. Amen.

Day 165

GOD WILL NEVER
FAIL TO LOVE YOU

*"You are a God of forgiveness, gracious and merciful,
slow to become angry, and rich in unfailing
love. You did not abandon them."*
NEHEMIAH 9:17 NLT

No matter what God's children did or how often they strayed,
God never abandoned them. As a pillar of cloud by day and of
fire by night, He continued to lead them. He continued to send
His Spirit to instruct them. He never stopped supplying heaven-
sent manna for their hunger and water for their thirst (see Nehemiah 9:19–20).

Your God has so much love for you that no matter how many
times you stray or rebel, He will continue to forgive, to be gracious
to you and show you mercy. His anger will be slow and temporary,
and He'll always love you. That's how much you matter to Him.

*Lord, I thank You for being so patient with me and
loving me no matter what. May I be as gracious,
patient, and loving toward others.*

REACH NEW HEIGHTS

*He gives power to the faint, and to him who has no might
he increases strength. Even youths shall faint and be weary,
and young men shall fall exhausted; but they who wait for the
Lord shall renew their strength; they shall mount up with wings like
eagles; they shall run and not be weary; they shall walk and not faint.*
Isaiah 40:29–31 esv

Do you greet the new day feeling renewed? Or are you left tired and ragged from the relentless demands of your daily schedule? Life today happens at high speed, and patience seems to have been scrapped from our makeup in favor of a more streamlined design. We want our food fast, our communication instant, and that new doodad we ordered delivered yesterday.

It isn't God's plan for you to merely trudge through the day. If you're worn thin, examine your activities and your priorities. Ask God for His input on your to-do list. Pause. Wait. Breathe in. Breathe out. Pray and be still.

*Father, teach me patience and trust
so I can rest in Your will. Amen.*

GOD MANIFESTS HIS POWERS AMID YOUR WEAKNESS

*My grace (My favor and loving-kindness and mercy) is
enough for you [sufficient against any danger and enables
you to bear the trouble manfully]; for My strength and
power are made perfect (fulfilled and completed) and
show themselves most effective in [your] weakness.*
2 CORINTHIANS 12:9 AMPC

The apostle Paul had a thorn in his side, some infirmity that
he wrestled with, so he pleaded for the Lord to rid him of it.
That's when Christ told Paul that His grace, love, kindness, and
mercy were all Paul needed to bear through whatever assailed
him. In fact, Christ's power showed itself even more effective
in Paul's weakness!

That response from Christ prompted Paul to write, "Therefore, I will all the more gladly glory in my weaknesses and
infirmities, that the strength and power of Christ (the Messiah)
may rest (yes, may pitch a tent over and dwell) upon me!"
(2 Corinthians 12:9 AMPC).

*I'm so amazed that I can endure anything and
everything when I have Your love, Lord! May Your
tent rest over me as a demonstration of Your power!*

TRY JESUS

*God, you did everything you promised, and I'm thanking
you with all my heart. You pulled me from the brink
of death, my feet from the cliff-edge of doom. Now I
stroll at leisure with God in the sunlit fields of life.*
PSALM 56:12–13 MSG

Isn't it exciting to share new solutions with others? Whether it's a "miracle" beauty cream or a delicious recipe, we love telling others about our discoveries. But why is it when Jesus is the solution to a problem, we see that we're much more hesitant to speak up? Why not share how His peace has soothed your anxiety or how His joy has cured your depression? Or how your anger has cooled in the refreshing pool of His grace?

Next time you see someone struggling, share with them the transforming power of walking through this life with Jesus as your constant companion.

Lord, may I be bold in sharing what You've done for me. Amen.

GOD RESTS YOUR SOUL

*Thus says the Lord, "Stand by the ways and see and
ask for the ancient paths, where the good way is,
and walk in it; and you will find rest for your souls."*
JEREMIAH 6:16 NASB

Jesus speaks about your soul, saying, "Take My yoke upon you
and learn from Me, for I am gentle and humble in heart, and
you will find rest for your souls" (Matthew 11:29 NASB). The latter
part of this verse is a direct quote from Jeremiah 6:16 above.

God's message is clear. In Him alone does your soul find
true rest. On His path alone, His good way, your soul finds the
relief, refreshment, quiet, and rest that it craves. Ask God to
show you His path. Walk it, and your soul will find its ease, no
matter what comes your way.

*I'm calling upon You today, Lord, to show me the good
way You would have me go. There my soul will find the
blessed quiet, the peace, and the rest it craves.*

TAKE A BREATHER

"Be still, and know that I am God. I will be exalted among the nations, I will be exalted in the earth!" The LORD of hosts is with us; the God of Jacob is our fortress.
PSALM 46:10–11 ESV

God wants you to take a time-out in all your self-important scampering about and listen. He often speaks in a whisper. So it's in the still hush of the pause that you will hear His voice. Our minds are usually rushing just as fast as our feet—scrolling through to-do lists and worries at landscape-blurring speeds, so even if we do still our bodies for a bit, our minds are far from rest.

Find a quiet, solitary place. Be still. Shush those rampant, anxiety-inducing thoughts. Listen. Meditate on scripture. Know that He is God—omniscient, powerful, unchanging. The realization will bring you peace and security, and maybe even a gentle reality check about your self-importance.

God, keep me humble. Speak into my stillness. Amen.

GOD TRANSFORMS YOUR MIND

Don't copy the behavior and customs of this world,
but let God transform you into a new person by changing
the way you think. Then you will learn to know God's will
for you, which is good and pleasing and perfect.
ROMANS 12:2 NLT

God wants you to allow Him to mold you into the person He created you to be, to change the way you think, to open your mind so that He can point you toward what He wills for you.

Your path to God's transformation of you begins with His Word, spending time in it, meditating on it. Doing so will renew your thoughts. It will also change your heart as you begin to know Him better, depend on and trust in Him more.

Your thoughts will be God-inspired, and you'll find your way as you follow their leading. You will find yourself moving at His impulses, not your own. And His way will become your way—good, pleasing, and perfect.

Show me Your way, Lord. Transform my mind,
change my heart, so that I find Your will and way for
my feet, a good, pleasing, and perfect path to follow.

Day 172
PRAY FIRST

If you don't know what you're doing, pray to the Father. He loves to help. You'll get his help, and won't be condescended to when you ask for it. Ask boldly, believingly, without a second thought.
JAMES 1:5–6 MSG

Friend, you don't need to wring your hands in worry when indecision plagues you. Pray! Are you struggling with a decision about your future? Ask Him. Do you need help learning how to connect with your kids? Ask Him. Are you in a strained relationship and can't figure out how to restore it? Ask Him.

Your Father in heaven gives His guidance generously and without condescension. He doesn't want you wandering around blind! Pray and search scripture for His wisdom. His Word is living and applicable to every part of your life. He wants you to have the answers you need to live within the bounds of His purpose for you. Just ask!

Father, may I come to You first for help
before I make mistakes. Amen.

GOD SURROUNDS YOU
WITH HIS POWER

*"Don't be afraid!" Elisha told him. "For there are more
on our side than on theirs!" Then Elisha prayed, "O Lord,
open his eyes and let him see!" The Lord opened the young
man's eyes, and when he looked up, he saw that the hillside
around Elisha was filled with horses and chariots of fire.*
2 KINGS 6:16–17 NLT

The king of Aram kept planning ambushes against Israel. But his
plans were continually thwarted by the prophet Elisha.

One day Elisha's servant awoke, went out, and was alarmed
by seeing the enemy army had surrounded the city with horses
and chariots. Panicked, he asked Elisha, "What will we do now?"
(2 Kings 6:15 NLT). Elisha told him not to be afraid, for they had
a greater army on their side. Then he prayed that God would
open his servant's eyes. When He did, the man saw God's horses
and chariots of fire.

You need never fear any "army" that comes against you,
because God has you surrounded by His heavenly power!

*Lord, I know I need fear nothing, for Your heavenly
power is all around me, shielding me from harm!
Thank You for Your heavenly protection!*

MORE LIKE HIM

If someone claims, "I know him well!" but doesn't keep his commandments, he's obviously a liar. His life doesn't match his words. But the one who keeps God's word is the person in whom we see God's mature love. This is the only way to be sure we're in God. Anyone who claims to be intimate with God ought to live the same kind of life Jesus lived.

1 JOHN 2:4–6 MSG

We belong to a holy God who asks us to be holy as He is holy. We were bought from sin by Jesus' precious blood and asked to walk like Jesus walked. Are you growing to be more and more like Him, to reflect the nature of the God you belong to?

You aren't going to be perfect. You're going to take a few missteps. But the more time you spend in the company of Jesus, the more your life will look like His. His gentle kindness, loving forgiveness, total joy, and unshakable peace will take up residence in your character.

Lord, teach me to follow in Your footsteps. Amen.

GOD WALKS WITH YOU AMID THE FIRE

*"Look! I see four men walking around in
the fire, unbound and unharmed, and the
fourth looks like a son of the gods."*
DANIEL 3:25 NIV

King Nebuchadnezzar sent for three men—Shadrach, Meshach,
and Abednego—who refused to worship a golden image he'd
made. Their punishment? Being tied up and thrown into a
fiery furnace.

The men had told the king, "God. . .is able to deliver us from
it. . . . But even if he does not. . .we will not serve your gods or
worship the image of gold you have set up" (Daniel 3:17–18 NIV).

When the king looked into the furnace, he saw a fourth
person with them, one who looked like a son of the gods! The
men were unharmed, their clothes intact, and not even the
smell of smoke on them! Because of their faith, Nebuchadnezzar
praised God.

God is with you—even when you walk through fire!

*Remind me all my days, Lord, of how You
stand with me when I stand up for You!*

Day 176

HE'S DELIGHTED WITH YOU

*The King of Israel, the L*ORD*, is in your midst; you shall never again*
fear evil. On that day it shall be said to Jerusalem: "Fear not, O Zion;
*let not your hands grow weak. The L*ORD *your God is in your midst,*
a mighty one who will save; he will rejoice over you with gladness;
he will quiet you by his love; he will exult over you with loud singing."
ZEPHANIAH 3:15–17 ESV

Does anyone like me? Who hasn't heard this insecure thought echo
in their mind? Even if we are surrounded by friends, we often
feel disliked and unaccepted.

The enemy will take this opportunity to whisper something
evil. He'll tell you that you're overlooked and unappreciated by
everyone. But God's Word says something different, something
hopeful and encouraging—something bright! Your heavenly
Father takes great delight in you! He loves you and rejoices over
you. He's so ecstatic when you enter into His presence that He
sings with joy when you arrive.

God, You're pleased to see me! Thank You
so much for Your tender care. Amen.

GOD'S WORD POINTS YOU TO SUCCESS

They went out and got into the boat, but that night they caught
nothing. . . . He [Jesus] said, "Throw your net on the right side
of the boat and you will find some." When they did, they were
unable to haul the net in because of the large number of fish.
JOHN 21:3, 6 NIV

After the resurrected Jesus had appeared to the disciples in the upper room, Simon Peter decided to go fishing. Several other disciples joined him. All night, they caught nothing. When dawn was breaking, Jesus was on the beach, although the men did not yet realize it was Him.

Jesus called out, asking if they'd caught any fish. When they said no, He told them to throw their net on the right side of the boat. When they did, their net was overflowing with fish!

Just as Jesus continued to care and provide for His followers, He continues to care and provide for you. His Word will always point you to the bounty that awaits. Simply follow His lead.

Lord, You always know and provide just what I need.
Help me stay alert to Your Word and obedient to Your
direction. You always point me to the bounty that awaits.

Day 178

GLORIOUSLY NEW

But there's far more to life for us. We're citizens of high heaven!
We're waiting the arrival of the Savior, the Master, Jesus Christ,
who will transform our earthy bodies into glorious bodies like his own.
He'll make us beautiful and whole with the same powerful skill by
which he is putting everything as it should be, under and around him.
PHILIPPIANS 3:21 MSG

Oh, what a day when we will receive our resurrection bodies! The Bible says that we'll be raised imperishable, glorious, and powerful (see 1 Corinthians 15:42–44). After His resurrection, Jesus did amazing things like appear and disappear, yet He could also eat and drink.

The Bible offers a glimpse of Jesus' return: "In a moment, in the twinkling of an eye, at the last trumpet. . .we shall be changed. For this perishable body must put on the imperishable, and this mortal body must put on immortality" (1 Corinthians 15:52–53 ESV).

Whatever we look like, the pain of this world will no longer plague us, and we'll be gloriously happy in His presence—forever!

God, I will be steadfast in my work for
You here because glory awaits! Amen.

Day 179

GOD CALLS YOU PRECIOUS

I have called you by your name; you are Mine. When you
pass through the waters, I will be with you, and through
the rivers, they will not overwhelm you. When you walk
through the fire, you will not be burned or scorched, nor will
the flame kindle upon you. For I am the Lord your God.
ISAIAH 43:1–3 AMPC

It's because of God's great love for you that He promises to walk
with you through any situation, challenge, trial, temptation,
or ordeal you may find yourself in. He'll be with you through
flooding waters and rapid rivers, keeping your head above the
water. If you find yourself walking amid flames, He will be with
you as He was with Shadrach, Meshach, and Abednego (see
Daniel 3). He is your loving God, and you are His precious
daughter.

So do not fear or doubt. Have courage and faith, knowing
God is with you through this life and beyond.

I feel so valued in Your eyes, Lord, for to You I am precious.
I put my hand in Yours, Father God. Let's walk!

ATTITUDE OF THANKSGIVING

*Be persistent and devoted to prayer, being alert and focused
in your prayer life with an attitude of thanksgiving.*
COLOSSIANS 4:2 AMP

Elaine muttered to herself and grabbed a cleaning rag. Some
days she felt like the maid. She swiped the sink clean just as her
phone chimed with a text. It was her prayer chain: PLEASE PRAY
FOR CHRISTIE. HER HUSBAND JUST DIED OF A HEART ATTACK.

Elaine gasped softly. Christie's husband was just a few years
older than her own. She immediately sat down on the side of
the tub to pray. Conviction about her poor attitude squeezed
her chest.

Friend, don't get stuck in a mud bog of complaining. An attitude of thanksgiving changes your perspective. It allows you to
name your blessings, look them in the face, and recognize God's
extravagant goodness.

Father, thank You for blessing me! Amen.

Day 181

GOD BLESSES AND MULTIPLIES YOUR OFFERING

Jesus took the five loaves and two fish, looked up toward heaven, and blessed them. . . . Afterward, the disciples picked up twelve baskets of leftover bread and fish. A total of 5,000 men and their families were fed.
MARK 6:41, 43–44 NLT

Jesus had just finished teaching a large crowd of people. The disciples suggested that Jesus send the people away so they could find some food to eat. But Jesus had other plans. He told the men to find whatever food they could in the crowd. What they found only amounted to five loaves of bread and two fish. But Jesus took the food and multiplied it—and not only was everyone fed, but there were leftovers!

When you bring whatever you have—even if it's just a little—to Jesus, He will bless it and multiply it for your benefit, the good of others, and His glory.

Lord, here's what I have to offer. Please bless it for Your glory!

PRECIOUS THOUGHTS

How precious to me are your thoughts, O God!
PSALM 139:17 ESV

We can control what we think. And we should! The enemy would set your focus on thoughts that will lead you away from God—fear, anxiety, bitterness, anger. But it's your choice what you will think about and who you will become: "For as he thinks in his heart, so is he" (Proverbs 23:7 AMP).

It's vital that you manage your mind and nurture it with wholesome, life-giving thoughts from God's Word. Try buckling your mind to God's way of thinking today: "Whatever is true, whatever is honorable, whatever is just, whatever is pure, whatever is lovely, whatever is commendable, if there is any excellence, if there is anything worthy of praise, think about these things" (Philippians 4:8 ESV).

God, I choose excellent, rejuvenating thoughts today
that will lead me into Your purpose for me. Amen.

GOD'S GIVEN WORD NEVER FAILS

With God nothing is ever impossible and no word from
God shall be without power or impossible of fulfillment.
LUKE 1:37 AMPC

When the angel Gabriel visited Mary, he had some astonishing news. She was to become the mother of the Son of God. Gabriel then told Mary her once-barren and aged cousin Elizabeth had also conceived and was already six months along! He ended these revelations by saying that nothing was impossible with God and no word of His ever failed.

To all this, Mary responded with, "Behold, I am the handmaiden of the Lord; let it be done to me according to what you have said" (Luke 1:38 AMPC).

Every ordinary girl can live an extraordinary life when she trusts in God, obeys His will, and believes nothing is impossible with God!

With You, Lord, nothing is impossible! Your powerful word
never fails! On these truths I base my faith and my life.

FORWARD INTO FREEDOM

"Why is the Lord bringing us into this land, to fall by the sword?
. . . Would it not be better for us to go back to Egypt?"
NUMBERS 14:3 ESV

Moses led the Israelites into freedom, but once they entered the wilderness all they could think about was how good it had been in Egypt. Their present difficulty had them looking back through rose-colored glasses at their previous slavery.

And how like us. Our fickle minds edit out the nasty parts of our former bondage to harsh masters like shame, fear, and addiction, and hoodwink us into craving the chains we just escaped. There's comfort in the familiar.

Be encouraged. Casting off old thought patterns and habits is hard. But God isn't leading you into the wilderness to stay. His plans for your life lead into the promised land of an abundant new life of freedom with God.

Father, help me to remember that Your plans
of freedom for me are in front, not behind.
They lie on the other side of the wilderness. Amen.

GOD IS YOUR PROTECTIVE WALL OF FIRE

" 'And I myself will be a wall of fire around it,'
declares the Lord, 'and I will be its glory within.' "
ZECHARIAH 2:5 NIV

God wants Himself and His words to be the wall of fire that surrounds you, protecting you. God and His Word are also the fire burning *within* you. When, after His resurrection, the at-first unrecognized Jesus left the two men traveling to Emmaus, they remarked to each other, "Were not our hearts greatly moved and burning within us while He was talking with us on the road and as He opened and explained to us [the sense of] the Scriptures?" (Luke 24:32 AMPC). And in Jeremiah 23:29 (NLT), God said, "Does not my word burn like fire?"

Allow God to set your life ablaze in this good way as you realize the blessings in your midst.

Lord, be my wall of fire without and the glory burning within!

A LIVING TESTIMONY

*"The reason I was born and came into
the world is to testify to the truth."*
JOHN 18:37 NIV

Jesus came to testify to the truth. He came to give us evidence of God's great plan for mankind: our sin, God's love, forgiveness through Jesus' death and resurrection, the Holy Spirit transforming our lives from within, and the hope of an eternal future with Him. Jesus is the evidence!

Your authentic life for God can make a difference too. As a follower of Jesus, you're called to testify about the changing power of God in your life. Live a real faith—one where you're honest about your struggles and about how God breaks through your problems. The world will notice that you're different, and your light will draw people to Jesus.

Lord, make my life a living testimony to Your truth. Amen.

GOD FAVORS
TENDER HEARTS

Never before had there been a king like Josiah, who turned to
the Lord with all his heart and soul and strength, obeying all the
laws of Moses. And there has never been a king like him since.
2 KINGS 23:25 NLT

Josiah became king when he was eight years old. Unlike many
kings before him, he followed the one true God. When the book
of law was found in the temple and read to Josiah, he tore his
clothes in despair. He sent his priests to discover the consequences of the people not having obeyed God's law. They found
a prophetess named Huldah who sent word to Josiah, "Because
your heart was [tender and] penitent and you humbled yourself
before the Lord. . .your eyes shall not see all the evil which I will
bring on this place" (2 Kings 22:19–20 AMPC).

Turn to God with a loving and tender heart, and you'll find
yourself greatly favored by God.

My tender heart is open to You, Lord. Speak, and I will humbly
serve and obey You with all my heart, strength, and soul.

THE PEACE OF BELONGING

"I have said these things to you, that in me you may
have peace. In the world you will have tribulation.
But take heart; I have overcome the world."
JOHN 16:33 ESV

Jesus said that living in this world would be hard. Sin reigns here, and we bleed under its iron fist of suffering. Death and disease, heartache and pain, fear and darkness—sometimes the ache of just being here feels like too much to bear. But then Jesus gave us hope: "In me you may have peace. . . . Take heart; I have overcome the world." *In Him.* Jesus is the only one who can bring tranquility to your soul—in Him your future is secure.

Jesus can calm whatever storm you're facing. When fear grips you, ask yourself if you truly think that your problem is bigger than God. There's peace beyond understanding when you belong to Him.

Lord, my troubles may be great, but You are greater. Amen.

GOD BROUGHT YOU TO THIS PLACE AND TIME

*If you keep silent at this time, relief and deliverance shall arise
for the Jews from elsewhere, but you and your father's house
will perish. And who knows but that you have come to the
kingdom for such a time as this and for this very occasion?*
ESTHER 4:14 AMPC

Esther was an orphaned Jewish girl who had been raised by
her cousin Mordecai. When King Ahasuerus began looking for
another queen, Esther, was the one he chose!

Sometime later, the king's evil official named Haman de-
vised a plan to have all the Jews killed. That's when Mordecai
sent word to Esther. She was their last hope to thwart Haman's
plans and save her people.

Just as God had a plan for Esther's life, He has a plan for
yours. God has brought you to this particular place and time to
live your life purpose. Trust Him, and He'll help you find your
way to bless His people.

*Show me, Lord, what You have brought me here to do.
I trust You to help me find Your path and purpose for me.*

Day 190

THE SWEET
PERFUME OF JESUS

*But thank God! He has made us his captives and continues to
lead us along in Christ's triumphal procession. Now he uses
us to spread the knowledge of Christ everywhere, like a sweet
perfume. Our lives are a Christ-like fragrance rising up to God. . . .
To those who are being saved, we are a life-giving perfume.*
2 Corinthians 2:14–16 nlt

After shivering for months under winter's harsh breath, you step
outside into the welcoming sunshine and inhale deeply the scent
of new life. Does your life smell as sweet to God? Does the fresh
scent of hope and belonging waft from your everyday actions?
As believers in Jesus, we are to be a life-giving perfume that
saturates the air around us with an irresistible aroma of hope.
This world is filled to the brim with repulsive, stinky attitudes.
People will notice if you step into the room with the lingering
scent of your Savior clinging to your thoughts and actions. They'll
want to know the name of the fragrance you're wearing. And
you can say *Jesus*!

*Father, may my actions today attract
people to Your life-giving Son. Amen.*

GOD SURROUNDS YOU WITH HIS SHIELD OF LOVE

Let all who take refuge in you rejoice; let them sing joyful
praises forever. Spread your protection over them, that all
who love your name may be filled with joy. For you bless the
godly, O Lord; you surround them with your shield of love.
PSALM 5:11–12 NLT

God won't just shower you with His love, He'll *shield* you with it. And because God Himself is the personification of love, it means that *He* is the one surrounding you, protecting you from head to toe.

There are so many benefits to trusting, running to, and relying on the God who created the entire universe and beyond. That's a lot of love, protection, and shielding. That's a lot of God! And He's doing it just for you!

Lord, I'm overwhelmed by the vastness of You and
Your love. I'm running to You now. Surround me
with Your shield of love as I trust in and cherish You!

TOGETHER FOREVER

*He will swallow up death forever. The Lord God will wipe away
all tears and take away forever all insults and mockery against
his land and people. The Lord has spoken—he will surely do it!*
ISAIAH 25:8 TLB

Heaven is going to be a fantastically wonderful place. Imagine
the undiluted joy of being with your loved ones and knowing it
will never end, of being in the unfiltered presence of our God.
Here on earth our love and joy are tainted by the fear of loss
and death; we fear the sharp prick of separation. Our greatest
sorrow began ages past in a garden when we were separated
from the Creator who loved us first and best. But God in His
unimaginable mercy has promised to remove this pall of separation and restore the joy of our fellowship forever!

*Father, You have given me the hope of
an eternal future without fear. Amen.*

GOD CONTINUALLY RESCUES YOU

*Daniel was brought and cast into the den of
lions. The king said to Daniel, May your God,
Whom you are serving continually, deliver you!*
DANIEL 6:16 AMPC

Daniel had been taken to Babylon, where he worked for three kings. King Darius was so impressed with Daniel's wisdom, trustworthiness, and ability that he put him in charge of the entire kingdom!

Some jealous officials coerced Darius into signing a law saying that those who prayed to anyone other than the king would be thrown into the lions' den. Soon Daniel, who diligently prayed three times a day to God, found himself in the lions' den, much to the king's dismay. Yet Daniel survived because God "sent His angel and has shut the lions' mouths" (Daniel 6:22 AMPC).

God rescues all those who serve, trust, and are faithful to Him.

*Thank You, Lord, for continuing to rescue me
as I stay faithful to You. I trust in You alone to
deliver me today, tomorrow, and forever!*

HIS COMPASSION

" 'He will wipe every tear from their eyes. There will
be no more death' or mourning or crying or pain,
for the old order of things has passed away."
REVELATION 21:4 NIV

God cares about your suffering. He sees you. He knows. He aches for you.

God is not only aware of your pain, but He is moved by it:

"I will be glad and rejoice in your love, for you saw my affliction and knew the anguish of my soul" (Psalm 31:7 NIV).

"In all their distress he too was distressed" (Isaiah 63:9 NIV).

He loves you deeply and feels your pain as if it were His own. Lean in to Jesus; He will give you strength.

This world is fallen, but God has promised that someday all our pain will be wiped away. In His eternal kingdom, suffering and death will be no more.

Father, redeem my pain for Your purpose. Amen.

Day 195

GOD EQUIPS YOU

*"You come to me with sword, spear, and javelin,
but I come to you in the name of the Lord of Heaven's
Armies...." So David triumphed over the Philistine
with only a sling and a stone, for he had no sword.*
1 Samuel 17:45, 50 nlt

When the shepherd boy David finally convinced King Saul that
the God who rescued him from lions and bears would rescue him
from the giant Goliath, the king gave David his own battle gear
to wear (see 1 Samuel 17:38 nlt). But after strapping the sword
over the borrowed armor, David could barely walk. So he took
it off. And "armed only with his shepherd's staff and sling, he
started across the valley to fight the Philistine" (1 Samuel 17:40
nlt). In the end, it was God's power, David's sling, faith, and
one stone that brought down the giant.

When challenged by the giants in your life, trust that God
has already equipped you with everything you need to triumph!

*I'm blessed to have You clothe and equip me in Your
power, Lord. As I trust in You, I'm ready to face any
challenge that comes before me—in Your name!*

WORSHIP IN WONDER

*The heavens declare the glory of God, and the sky
above proclaims his handiwork. . . . Their voice goes
out through all the earth, and their words to the end
of the world. In them he has set a tent for the sun.*

PSALM 19:1, 4 ESV

Have you ever laid on your back under an endless blanket of glittering stars and allowed the wonder to creep into your soul? Have your thoughts drifted to the one who made it?

If you have never done this, grab a comfy blanket and steal out into the dark on the next clear night. Lay back and rest in awe of His eternal power. Worship Him for His limitless creativity, care, and attention to this world He called into being. Know that He knows you. The great one who drew sparkling pictures in the vastness of our universe loves you with all the greatness of His being.

*Lord God, I am a small speck, like one of those pinpoints of light
among the billions, but You know my name. You know every detail
about me down to the number of hairs on my head. You see me
amid the masses. And You love me as if I were the only one. Amen.*

GOD ESPECIALLY BLESSES YOU—FOR YOU'VE NOT SEEN YET STILL BELIEVE!

*Then Jesus told him, "You believe because you have seen
me. Blessed are those who believe without seeing me."*
JOHN 20:29 NLT

When the disciples told Thomas they'd seen Jesus, he said, "I
won't believe it unless I see the nail wounds in his hands, put
my fingers into them, and place my hand into the wound in his
side" (John 20:25 NLT).

Eight days later, Jesus appeared to the disciples again, and
Thomas was with them. Jesus told him to put his finger in His
wounds. And Thomas did, prompting Jesus to tell him, "You
believe because you have seen me. Blessed are those who believe
without seeing me."

You, woman, have believed without needing to see the physical evidence. You believe Jesus at His word. Your sown confidence
reaps Jesus' blessing—now and forevermore!

*I do believe, Jesus! You're my Savior. I believe You at Your word
and see You through Your Word. That seeing is my believing!*

COMMIT TO YOUR CALLING

*Jonah ran away from the LORD and headed
for Tarshish. He went down to Joppa,
where he found a ship bound for that port.*
JONAH 1:3 NIV

Jonah knew exactly what it feels like to be asked by God to do something that you don't want to do. He didn't like it, and he didn't like the people God was sending him to. It's easy to obey when what we're asked to do lines up with our own interests; but being faithful is much more difficult when obedience is costly.

God has plans for you, friend, but faithfulness to His ways is key to living in His purpose—even in the little things.

If you've hopped a boat that's speeding in the opposite direction, turn back now. Welcome His purpose into your life.

God, keep me committed to Your calling, no matter what. Amen.

Day 199

GOD CARRIES YOU
IN HIS ARMS

GOD, the Master, comes in power, ready to go into action.
He is going to pay back his enemies and reward those who
have loved him. Like a shepherd, he will care for his flock,
gathering the lambs in his arms, hugging them as he carries
them, leading the nursing ewes to good pasture.
ISAIAH 40:10–11 MSG

The same Lord who comes in power to defend you cares for you like a loving and gentle shepherd. Because you have faith in Him and love Him, He who protects you and shields you from all dangers is longing to reward you.

God reaches out and picks up the weakest in His flock. He hugs these lambs to Himself as He carries them along. While He walks, He leads the nursing mothers to a good pasture, where they can find the fuel that will help them take care of the little lambs.

Today, trust that God is carrying you when you are weary and leading you to nourishment when you need strength.

Thank You for lifting me up, Lord, when I'm
weary, loving me, hugging me, protecting me,
nourishing me. I yield to Your gentle hand.

KEEP DOING GOOD

*Whoever sows to please the Spirit, from the Spirit will reap
eternal life. Let us not become weary in doing good, for at
the proper time we will reap a harvest if we do not give up.
Therefore, as we have opportunity, let us do good to all people,
especially to those who belong to the family of believers.*
GALATIANS 6:8–10 NIV

We're here to sow seeds of faith and love and good deeds that
benefit others around us. God knows a servant's heart can get
tired, especially when our efforts go unnoticed and unappreciated. He encourages us through scripture: Don't get tired of
doing good! Your rewards are up ahead!

Don't pass up any opportunity to do good for someone today!
Don't let the enemy tell you your efforts are wasted—for you
will reap an eternal harvest. Don't give up. Keep teaching your
children about Jesus. Keep loving the hard to love. Keep encouraging the downhearted. Just keep swimming, friend!

*Lord, may I work diligently to please
Your Spirit in this life. Amen.*

GOD NEVER DISAPPOINTS YOU

*In my distress I prayed to the LORD, and the LORD answered me
and set me free. The LORD is for me, so I will have no fear. . . .
It is better to take refuge in the LORD than to trust in people.
It is better to take refuge in the LORD than to trust in princes.*
PSALM 118:5–6, 8–9 NLT

It may be hard to imagine, but there will be people you trust who
will, at some time, disappoint you. It may be a family member
who doesn't come through on a promise. A friend who passed
your secret on to someone else. A coworker who said something
behind your back.

The psalmist makes clear that it's better to take refuge in and
trust in God than in people or princes. "No man who believes in
Him [who adheres to, relies on, and trusts in Him] will [ever]
be put to shame or be disappointed" (Romans 10:11 AMPC). Trust
in God. He'll be there every time, true to His word.

*I feel safe, secure, and loved in You, Lord.
You never let me down. It's in You alone I'll trust.*

Day 202
KNOWING HIS WILL

We do not know what we ought to pray for, but the Spirit himself
intercedes for us through wordless groans. And he who searches
our hearts knows the mind of the Spirit, because the Spirit
intercedes for God's people in accordance with the will of God.
And we know that in all things God works for the good of those
who love him, who have been called according to his purpose.
ROMANS 8:26–28 NIV

If you're struggling to understand God's plan for your life, know
that as a loving Father, God gives you options within His will
as well—all of which are equally pleasing to Him. You choose.

Romans 8:26–28 tells us that God works for the good of *those*
who love Him. If your heart is turned toward God in love and sub-
mission, He can use you in whichever option you choose. And
when you're struggling with making a choice, He promises the
Holy Spirit will pray for you in accordance with God's will. Love
God. Walk in His Word. And His plan will be revealed day by day.

Heavenly Father, I give my decisions to You. Amen.

Day 203

GOD HELPS YOU, HOLDING YOUR RIGHT HAND

"Don't be afraid, for I am with you. Don't be discouraged,
for I am your God. I will strengthen you and help you. I will
hold you up with my victorious right hand. . . . For I hold you
by your right hand—I, the LORD your God. And I say to you,
'Don't be afraid. I am here to help you. . . . I will help you.'"
ISAIAH 41:10, 13–14 NLT

Through Isaiah, God could not have made it any clearer. He wants you to know you're never to be anxiously looking around. He assures you that you need not be afraid because He—the Source, Provider, Creator, Redeemer, Refuge, and Fortress—is right here with you.

God has you by your right hand. He's speaking to you, saying "Don't fear anything. I'm here to help. YOU WILL BE HELPED!"

Picture yourself being lifted in God's right hand while He holds your right. Hear His voice telling you not to fear. See all things coming against you as dust. What a picture of a God who loves you with all His might!

Lord, I hear You! You are all the help and strength I need!

Day 204

NEAR TO GOD

My flesh and my heart may fail, but God is the strength of my heart and my portion forever. For behold, those who are far from you shall perish; you put an end to everyone who is unfaithful to you. But for me it is good to be near God; I have made the Lord GOD my refuge, that I may tell of all your works.

PSALM 73:26–28 ESV

Sometimes walking close with the Lord can be a little uncomfortable. He asks hard things of us. Love when you'd rather not. Exercise self-control. Wait. Be gentle. Show kindness. It's easy to look at the ungodly and think that their lives are easy, smooth-sailing fun. But God has revealed their ultimate end to us—eternal separation from Him.

The writer of Psalm 73 concluded that even though the worldly people around him seemed to be living high on the hog at the moment, he would rather be near God. We have one of two destinations: nearness with God or separation. Draw close to Him, beloved. Crawl into His lap in spite of earthly trials.

Heavenly Father, keep me close. I desire faithfulness over momentary fun. Amen.

GOD GIVES YOU A NEW SONG TO SING

He has given me a new song to sing, a hymn of praise to our God. . . . Oh, the joys of those who trust the Lord. . . . May all who search for you be filled with joy and gladness in you.
PSALM 40:3, 4, 16 NLT

God has put a new song of praise in your mouth. Why not sing that worship song to Him as soon as your eyes open in the morning? When you do, you'll be sure to begin your day seeing things from God's perspective. You'll be reaffirming how much you're loved, cared for, protected, and looked out for by your mighty Lord. To begin, try singing "I Will Sing of the Mercies of the Lord Forever," a song based on Psalm 89:1. It's an easy one to learn if you don't already know it. Even better, make up one of your own! Either way, the song of praise you sing to God will spark the flame of unsurpassable joy within—and without.

You've given me a song to sing, Lord. May the words from my mouth and the tune from my heart be pleasing to You, the one so deserving of praise.

SOW SEEDS OF THE SPIRIT

*What a person plants, he will harvest. The person who plants
selfishness, ignoring the needs of others—ignoring God!—harvests
a crop of weeds. All he'll have to show for his life is weeds!
But the one who plants in response to God, letting God's Spirit
do the growth work in him, harvests a crop of real life, eternal life.*

GALATIANS 6:7–8 MSG

Both in gardening and in life, we'll reap what we sow. You can't
plant seeds of selfishness and expect to harvest godliness. Want
to enjoy the beautiful blossoms of a real life with God here and
now and an amazing eternity with Him forever? Don't ignore
God. Instead look for His movements in the world around you
and join in! Grab that pouch of seeds and start sowing. But be
sure to scatter seeds born of the Spirit: love, joy, peace, patience,
kindness, goodness, faithfulness, and self-control. You won't be
disappointed with your crop!

*Lord, may I be conscious of my actions and attitudes.
Mold me to be more like You. Amen.*

GOD ENABLES YOU

*"I'm sending you to Pharaoh to bring my people, the People
of Israel, out of Egypt." Moses answered God, "But why me?
What makes you think that I could ever go to Pharaoh and lead
the children of Israel out of Egypt?" "I'll be with you," God said.*
EXODUS 3:10–12 MSG

When Moses encountered God speaking out of a burning bush,
he learned what God was calling him to do: bring His people out
of Egypt. Moses' first response was, "Why me? What makes you
think this is even something I can do?" God simply answered,
"No worries. I'll be with you."

When God gives you a calling, He also enables you to fulfill it
by equipping you with His presence, power, and words. And He
provides all the tools you'll need. With God, you are more than
good enough to do anything, for He is with you.

*Thank You, Lord, for making me more than good enough
to do what You are calling me to do. With Your presence,
power, and words, I cannot and will not fail.*

LIVE IN HIS LOVE

*"The LORD your God is in your midst, a mighty one who will
save; he will rejoice over you with gladness; he will quiet you
by his love; he will exult over you with loud singing."*
ZEPHANIAH 3:17 ESV

We want to be wanted. We long to be loved and accepted, to belong. But the people around us are just as sin-blighted as we are. Looking for the love you desire in a rotting world will leave you unsatisfied.

But God says that He will quiet you with His love. He can soothe your anxious and wounded worry over that coworker's glare or your friend's snappish response. Because He loves you. Every last, imperfect, slightly insecure inch of you.

Live in His love. Don't solicit it from another inferior source. His affection is not based on our effort. He loves you because you are His—His good and masterful creation.

*Lord, thank You for the soul-satisfying knowledge that I am
loved by You. Now I am free to give love away. Amen.*

GOD MAKES YOUR DAY

This is the day the LORD has made.
We will rejoice and be glad in it.
PSALM 118:24 NLT

Today, if you keep your heart tender, you will hear God's voice telling you the way you should go (see Hebrews 3:7–8). If you keep your eyes open, you will see God opening doors before you (see Revelation 3:8). If you stay close to God's Word, you will see how much He favors you, the loving daughter He knows by name (see Exodus 33:17). You may even encounter something God has been planning for you all along, something He has prepared that is beyond what you could ever have imagined (see 1 Corinthians 2:9).

Begin your day trusting in the one who makes your day, and you will find yourself rejoicing at everything that comes your way!

I am thrilled to be with You, Lord, on this new day
You have made! I will rejoice and be so glad in it!

LONGING FOR HIS COMPANY

*Christ, having been offered once to bear the sins of
many, will appear a second time, not to deal with sin
but to save those who are eagerly waiting for him.*
HEBREWS 9:28 ESV

Do we, as believers, crave the appearance of Jesus and long for His coming? Paul wrote to the Philippians that "many. . .walk as enemies of the cross of Christ. Their end is destruction, their god is their belly, and they glory in their shame, with minds set on earthly things" (Philippians 3:18–19 ESV). Often we too spend most of our day distracted by earthly concerns.

But how wonderful if our thoughts are continually bent toward heaven with an attitude of expectancy. No doubt our desires for earthly pleasures and sins would fade if our longings are pinned on our desire to be in the company of our friend, our Savior.

*Jesus, I crave Your coming. I'm eagerly waiting
for something so much better than this life.
I'm waiting to see Your face. Amen.*

GOD COMMANDS HIS ANGELS TO GUARD YOU

If you say, "The Lord is my refuge," and you make the
Most High your dwelling, no harm will overtake you,
no disaster will come near your tent. For he will command
his angels concerning you to guard you in all your ways.
PSALM 91:9–11 NIV

When you put yourself under God's care, relying on Him during difficulties and dangers, trusting He will protect you, and actively communing with Him, no harm can come to you. You will be covered by His holy and supreme presence. But that's not all. When you admit that God is indeed your refuge, He will order His angels to guard you. He bids them to secure your safety, to be a shield to your body, soul, and spirit. When you walk in God's way, God's angels keep you in your way. They are heaven-sent protection from a God who adores you. Is there any greater love?

Once again, Lord, I find myself speechless. There are
so many ways You care for me as I dwell beneath Your
wings. Thank You so much for the gift of Your angels.

ABIDE IN HIS REST

*"Come to me, all who labor and are heavy laden, and I will
give you rest. Take my yoke upon you, and learn from me,
for I am gentle and lowly in heart, and you will find rest for
your souls. For my yoke is easy, and my burden is light."*
MATTHEW 11:28–30 ESV

Jesus can take your burdens. With the power of a promise, He
gives rest to souls stomped into the mud of this sin-stained
world. He came to earth born as a human and proved to us that
He is powerful enough to back up His word. Believe in all that
He says He can do for you, and trust in His good future for you.
That trust will stir the winds of hope to lift your weak soul from
the slop of this world.

Come to Jesus, believe, abide in Him, and follow in His steps.
You will find the soul-rest of hope.

*Jesus, I believe You are the Christ. I give You my yoke in
exchange for rest. Teach me to abide in You. Amen.*

GOD GIVES YOU TRANQUILITY OF MIND AND SLEEP

In peace I will both lie down and sleep, for You, Lord,
alone make me dwell in safety and confident trust.
PSALM 4:8 AMPC

In Psalm 4, King David shares his formula for acquiring a good night's rest. It begins with a prayer to God. He remembers how God has freed him from his troubles. He affirms how the Lord sets apart the godly. How God listens when they speak to Him. David reminds himself to be still before God. He asks God to smile upon him and remembers the abundant joy God gives him.

At the end, David is ready to lie down and sleep, telling God (and in the process, himself) that it is He alone who makes him dwell in safety.

God wants you to have the same peace of mind when you are ready to say good night!

Lord, I want to fall asleep remembering it is You alone
who makes me safe. That You listen when I speak,
hear and answer my prayers, and smile down upon me.
You are my joy as I fall asleep in Your protective arms.

Day 214
YOU'VE GOT THE JOY

Dear friends, don't be surprised at the fiery trials you are going through, as if something strange were happening to you. Instead, be very glad—for these trials make you partners with Christ in his suffering, so that you will have the wonderful joy of seeing his glory when it is revealed to all the world.
1 PETER 4:12–13 NLT

Paul knew a secret: "I have learned in whatever situation I am to be content. I know how to be brought low, and I know how to abound. In any and every circumstance, I have learned the secret of facing plenty and hunger, abundance and need" (Philippians 4:11–12 ESV). But the next verse is the powerhouse of his contentment: "I can do all things through him who strengthens me" (Philippians 4:13 ESV).

The strength of Jesus fueled his contentment, and the hope of Jesus fueled his joy! No circumstance in this life could conquer his joy. He could live in prosperity or need because though he resided here for a time, his citizenship was in heaven.

Lord, fuel my joy with the knowledge
that heaven awaits! Amen.

GOD WANTS TO HEAR— AND GRANT—YOUR DESIRE

"What do you want me to do for you?" Jesus asked.
"My Rabbi," the blind man said, "I want to see!"
MARK 10:51 NLT

A blind man named Bartimaeus cried out, asking Jesus to have mercy on him. When Jesus heard Bartimaeus, He stopped and told the others to tell the man to come to Him. Hearing that Jesus was calling him, Bartimaeus threw off his coat and ran to Him.

When his desire was made clear, Jesus told Bartimaeus it was his faith that had healed him. At that instant, the blind man could see!

God wants you to tell Him exactly what you desire. It's not that He doesn't already know; It's that it brings Him joy to hear His beloved's request, and it's good for you to put it into words, having faith it will be granted.

Lord, I'm Your beloved. Let me tell
You from the heart what I desire.

GOD OF GLORIOUS RICHES

My God will supply every need of yours
according to his riches in glory in Christ Jesus.
PHILIPPIANS 4:19 ESV

Perspective is a powerful thing. Is your generosity fueled by an attitude of poverty or plenty? If you're tempted to hold back, remember that the God of the universe, who takes care of you and supplies your resources, fills your earthly basket from His limitless storehouse of glorious riches. Don't fear that God's resources are going to dry up! You can't out-give God's ability to bless you.

It's not merely money that we hoard. Be generous with your time, your love, your patience, your joy, your goodness. Give today because you are overflowing with God's bountiful blessings to you.

Heavenly Father, fuel my generosity with the knowledge
that Your storehouse will never empty. Amen.

GOD GIVES POWER TO THE FAINT WHO WAIT

*Those who wait for the Lord [who expect, look for, and hope
in Him] shall change and renew their strength and power;
they shall lift their wings and mount up [close to God] as
eagles [mount up to the sun]; they shall run and not be
weary, they shall walk and not faint or become tired.*
ISAIAH 40:31 AMPC

God never runs out of strength or energy. He is the all-powerful
and mighty God. Yet He knows that His people—young and old—
can run themselves down, can burn out, trying to do all they feel
they need or wish to do.

When you desperately need energy and strength, when
you're about to faint from exhaustion, go to God. He'll give you
power and give you abundant strength. Your job is to wait on
Him to do so, to look for and expect Him to reenergize you. He'll
reward your patience by renewing you. Trust Him to give you
the strength to fly like an eagle, mounting up ever closer to God.

*I'm so tired, Lord. I'm looking and expecting strength and power
from You, in Your time. You alone can renew me—mind, body,
spirit, and soul—so I can soar like the eagle, close to You.*

SPREAD THE KNOWLEDGE OF JESUS

Through us, he brings knowledge of Christ.
Everywhere we go, people breathe in the exquisite fragrance.
Because of Christ, we give off a sweet scent rising to God.
2 CORINTHIANS 2:14–15 MSG

If you're walking through the market and you catch a whiff of delicious chocolate cake wafting from the bakery, it can stop you in your tracks. On the flip side, the eye-watering stench of open sewage will force you back like the opposite pole of a magnet. But when the stink is masked by pleasant things, something bad can seem inviting. Some people are drawn to the aroma of a horse barn where the pungent smell of manure is mixed with the more pleasing fragrance of hay and grain. Sin can be like this too. And before you know it, you're knee-deep in something putrid.

When we spread the knowledge of Jesus, it is a sweet fragrance to God. He inhales deeply the pleasant aroma of His followers.

Heavenly Father, keep my feet from being
drawn to sin. In Jesus' name, amen.

GOD, THROUGH HIS WORD, PREPARES YOU FOR YOUR TASKS

Every part of Scripture is God-breathed and useful one way or another—showing us truth, exposing our rebellion, correcting our mistakes, training us to live God's way. Through the Word we are put together and shaped up for the tasks God has for us.
2 TIMOTHY 3:16–17 MSG

God has not left you alone to find your way in the dark. He has left His Word for you to read, study, and meditate on. This God-breathed text shows you the truth you need to live by. His Word shapes you, reforms you, equips you so that you can take on the tasks He has assigned to you.

As you trust in God and study His Word, you'll become inspired as you follow His direction and instruction. You'll gain wisdom as you ask the Holy Spirit to help you apply the scriptures to your life.

God's light continues to shine on you from His Word. Allow it to illuminate your life!

Holy Spirit, teach me how to apply my Lord's Word to my life. Show me what You would have me know as I open its pages today.

VICTORY BELONGS TO YOU

*Now Jericho was shut up inside and outside because of
the people of Israel. None went out, and none came in.
And the LORD said to Joshua, "See, I have given Jericho
into your hand, with its king and mighty men of valor."*

JOSHUA 6:1–2 ESV

The first time God had led His people to the promised land's
border, they hadn't trusted Him to deliver. Now it was time for
round two. God said, "See, I have given Jericho into your hand."

He instructed them to march around the walls, blowing
trumpets and shouting, and then the six-foot-thick walls of
Jericho would fall. This time they were ready to trust. God declared victory over the city before the walls even fell.

Maybe you are in the midst of scary circumstances in your
life—maybe you've lost your health, or a loved one, or your sense
of security. Don't fear, beloved. God is already there ahead of you.
And Jesus has declared victory over your life. Trust Him today.

*Lord, Your ability to do what You say is
absolute. Give me greater trust. Amen.*

GOD HAS AN UNBREAKABLE HOLD ON YOU

Listen to the L<small>ORD</small> who created you. . . . "Do not be afraid,
for I have ransomed you. I have called you by name; you are
mine. . . . From eternity to eternity I am God. No one can snatch
anyone out of my hand. No one can undo what I have done."
I<small>SAIAH</small> 43:1, 13 <small>NLT</small>

Listen up! God commands you to have no fear—of anything. He has saved you in a big way. You're safe in His hands, under His protection. Jesus has paid the ransom for your life, spirit, and soul.

God not only knows your name; He calls you by it. You're now His eternal possession. No one can ever snatch you away from Him. No matter what your circumstances are, He can and will deliver you out of them and bring you safely back to His loving arms. No devil, no evil, no man, no woman, no army, no king can come between you and God and His plans for you.

I have no fear for You are near, Lord,
and always will be. Amen!

SPEAK HIS WORDS

*"So is my word that goes out from my mouth: It will not
return to me empty, but will accomplish what I desire
and achieve the purpose for which I sent it."*
ISAIAH 55:11 NIV

God demonstrated the stunning creative power of His words in the Garden of Eden when He spoke and the world snapped into existence from the void. Jesus is called "the Word"—the creative force of God's voice. When God speaks, people are changed.

If you believe that Jesus came to this earth to redeem you from the darkness, forgive your sins, and save your eternal soul, you belong to God. You are indwelt with His Holy Spirit. He wants you to listen for His still, small voice and for you to speak His words. Speak Spirit-inspired words that build up, encourage, and comfort those around you. Ask the Holy Spirit to speak His uplifting words into your life today.

*Lord, I'm listening for Your Spirit.
Speak words of life to me. Amen.*

GOD TURNS CURSES INTO BLESSINGS FOR YOU

*"The LORD your God refused to listen to Balaam.
He turned the intended curse into a blessing
because the LORD your God loves you."*
DEUTERONOMY 23:5 NLT

When Balak, the king of Moab, saw the seemingly undefeatable Israelites camping near him, he was afraid they'd attack him and his people, so he offered riches to a man named Balaam in exchange for his cursing the Israelites. But Balaam told Balak he'd say only what God told him to say. And "God turned the curse into a blessing" (Nehemiah 13:2 NLT). (For the full story, check out Numbers 22–24.)

God says, "No weapon that is formed against you will prosper" (Isaiah 54:17 NASB) because "the LORD your God loves you."

So, the next time something unwarranted comes your way, don't panic. Stand strong in God. He will turn everything that happens in your life into a blessing!

*Lord, You are so good to me. I am comforted, encouraged,
and strengthened in the knowledge that You will turn all
things that fill me with dread, alarm, or fear into a blessing!
And all because You love me so much. Thank You, Lord.*

WALK IN HIS POWER

He said to me, "My grace is sufficient for you, for my power is made perfect in weakness." Therefore I will boast all the more gladly of my weaknesses, so that the power of Christ may rest upon me.
2 Corinthians 12:9 esv

You may think that God cannot use you, that the brokenness that litters your past disqualifies you or that your weaknesses render you ineffective. But those are Satan's lies to you.

Friend, you're giving your flaws too much credit. The living God of the universe is bigger than whatever weakness is debilitating you. God has all the power. And He told the apostle Paul, "My power is made perfect in weakness."

Yes, we are weak. Yes, we are flawed. But we are not without hope. We are not unusable. Share about your limitations and experience the power of Christ as the Holy Spirit accomplishes God's work through you, all the more gloriously because of your weakness.

*God, I give You myself. I can do nothing on
my own. May I move in Your power. Amen.*

GOD WILL NEVER FORGET YOU

"Can a woman forget her nursing child and have no compassion on the son of her womb? Even these may forget, but I will not forget you. Behold, I have inscribed you on the palms of My hands."
Isaiah 49:15–16 nasb

Nursing mothers are very attentive and attuned to their babies. It's as if the mothers have an invisible cord linking them to their child.

In today's verse, God makes it clear that He is even more attentive to you and has more compassion for you than a nursing mother! That although she may forget about you, He never will! He has your name tattooed on His hands.

No matter how neglected, forgotten, or abandoned you may feel by people—including your mother—rest assured that God will never, ever forget you. He is linked to you by the invisible cord of love.

Once more, Lord, You have taken my breath away. No one loves me as much as You do. With You I know I have a true home, now and forever. In You I rest, trust, and find true peace.

Day 226

PROTECTION FROM PRIDE

*I know a man in Christ who fourteen years ago was caught
up to the third heaven—whether in the body or out of the
body I do not know, God knows. And I know that this man
was caught up into paradise. . .and he heard things that
cannot be told, which man may not utter. . . . So to keep me
from becoming conceited because of the surpassing greatness
of the revelations, a thorn was given me in the flesh.*
2 Corinthians 12:2–4, 7 esv

The apostle Paul was given an extravagant revelation—he experienced the paradise of heaven! His experience was so awesome that God had to keep his head from swelling. So God gave him a thorn. . .something to wake him up to the reality of his circumstances—a sinful human in need of Jesus.

Humility is seeing yourself clearly. If you stay in touch with your limitations, you won't be tempted to think a bit too much of yourself. We cannot enter into God's kingdom without recognizing our need for Him. How can your limitations lead you into a renewed humility and dependence on God?

Father, forgive me if I have operated in pride. Amen.

Day 227

GOD WILL TURN THINGS
AROUND FOR YOU

"When you come looking for me, you'll find me.
Yes, when you get serious about finding me and want
it more than anything else, I'll make sure you won't be
disappointed. . . . I'll turn things around for you."
JEREMIAH 29:13–14 MSG

This world is full of distractions. And they may even cause your focus to shift away from God. Before you know it, although you're still routinely doing your devotions, saying brief prayers, and going to church on Sunday. . .you're more caught up in the world than you are in God.

That's when you need to go looking *for* God, to desire Him above all other things. When you do begin seeking God—with all your heart—you won't be disappointed. On the contrary, He'll start turning things around for you, getting your life and trust in Him back on track—to your good and His glory!

I'm not sure what happened, Lord, but I've gotten so caught
up in the world that I have stopped seeking Your wisdom,
knowledge, power, and strength. Help me get back on
track, God, because my life without You is a dead end.

FACE-TO-FACE ENCOUNTER

"For this is the covenant that I will make with the house of Israel after those days, declares the LORD: I will put my law within them, and I will write it on their hearts. And I will be their God, and they shall be my people. And no longer shall each one teach his neighbor and each his brother, saying, 'Know the LORD,' for they shall all know me, from the least of them to the greatest, declares the LORD. For I will forgive their iniquity, and I will remember their sin no more."
JEREMIAH 31:33–34 ESV

Becoming a believer is not about following rules carved in stone. It's loving a living God who loves you back and doing life with Him. "Whenever, though, they turn to face God as Moses did, God removes the veil and there they are—face-to-face! They suddenly recognize that God is a living, personal presence, not a piece of chiseled stone" (2 Corinthians 3:16–17 MSG).

Talk to Him. Spend time in His presence. Read about Him in His Word. Still yourself and listen for His voice. He wants conversation and participation in your life. "Those who trust God's action in them find that God's Spirit is in them—living and breathing God!" (Romans 8:5 MSG).

Holy Spirit, I invite You to speak to me today. In Jesus' name, amen.

Day 229

GOD MAKES EVERYTHING RIGHT FOR YOU

God makes everything come out right; he puts victims back on their feet.... God's love, though, is ever and always, eternally present to all who fear him, making everything right for them and their children as they follow his Covenant ways and remember to do whatever he said.

PSALM 103:6, 17–18 MSG

God knows you may need time to lick your wounds and rebuild your courage after a breakup, a loss, a rejection, or a physical ailment. So, when you're feeling discouraged, thinking you'll never find your soul mate, recover from a loved one's passing, recoup confidence, or regain your physical strength, don't worry. God will make everything come out right in His time. As you're walking with Him, God will rebuild, soothe, and comfort you. Then one day, before you're even aware of it, you'll find yourself back in the saddle, riding along as if you'd never fallen in the first place.

Lord, all the things I'd thought I'd never have or do again are within reach once more. Thank You for Your smooth hand in my life!

LOVE LETTER

You show that you are a letter from Christ delivered by us,
written not with ink but with the Spirit of the living God,
not on tablets of stone but on tablets of human hearts.
2 CORINTHIANS 3:3 ESV

Receiving letters is fun. The Bible says that *you* are a letter! A letter from Christ penned by the Holy Spirit to everyone you come in contact with. God's Spirit is written on your heart. He wants His transforming power to spill out of you in encouragement and hope just as the welcome words of a dear friend's letter. His life is written on your life!

What words are penned by the way you are living? Does Jesus' love, grace, and kindness speak from your attitudes and actions in a fervent letter to His beloved? If not, ask Him to transform you into a love letter to the world.

Jesus, may my life be living proof of Your
regenerating love. In Jesus' name, amen.

Day 231

GOD KNOWS AND BLESSES YOU

As high as heaven is over the earth, so strong is his love to those who fear him. . . . As parents feel for their children, GOD feels for those who fear him. He knows us inside and out, keeps in mind that we're made of mud.
PSALM 103:11, 13 MSG

God loves you more than words can ever express. He knows you inside and out. He realizes you're made of dust and that your body is a temporal structure. That your thoughts are not as high as His. Yet, because of Jesus, there is no separation from God and His love for you. There is no sin that's confessed that can stand between you and Him.

God is a father more loving, powerful, and wise than any earthly parent. He pardons all your wrongdoing, heals you, pulls you out of the pit, crowns you with love and compassion, and satisfies you with so many good things (see Psalm 103:2–5).

Even with all You know about me, Lord, You love me like no other. Bless the Lord, O my soul, as I seek to know and love Him more and more.

TRANSFORMED IN GLORY

Whenever anyone turns to the Lord, the veil is taken away.
Now the Lord is the Spirit, and where the Spirit of the Lord is,
there is freedom. And we all, who with unveiled faces contemplate
the Lord's glory, are being transformed into his image with ever-
increasing glory, which comes from the Lord, who is the Spirit.
2 CORINTHIANS 3:16–18 NIV

Jesus has ripped away the shroud of our broken relationship
with God: "Let us come boldly to the throne of our gracious God"
(Hebrews 4:16 NLT). We now live in the freedom of His life—the
freedom to behold His glory and to walk with Him again in conversation, the freedom to experience a transformation!

This change isn't a one-time event. Instead we become more
like His image with ever-increasing glory! "I am certain that God,
who began the good work within you, will continue his work
until it is finally finished on the day when Christ Jesus returns"
(Philippians 1:6 NLT).

God, as I look upon Your glory, change me.
May my soul shine radiantly with the
borrowed brightness of Your Son. Amen.

GOD HAS BLESSED YOU WITH DIVINE POWER

His divine power has granted to us everything pertaining to life and godliness, through the true knowledge of Him who called us by His own glory and excellence. For by these He has granted to us His precious and magnificent promises, so that by them you may become partakers of the divine nature.

2 PETER 1:3–4 NASB

Some days you may find yourself uncertain as to what God would have you do or what His plan is for your life. Yet you need not worry. Simply allow Jesus to live His life through you, to understand He's already given you all you need to become more like Him.

Jesus has made you promises. One of them is that because you believe in Him, He now lives in you. That means you have a share in His divine nature and that anything is possible. Your job is to keep living in Jesus, listening for His voice, and drinking in His Word.

Lord, sometimes I feel like I should be further along in my faith walk. Help me always remember that Jesus is in You, I am in Jesus, and Jesus is in me. So nothing is impossible!

KINDNESS COUNTS

When the goodness and loving kindness of God our Savior
appeared, he saved us, not because of works done by us in
righteousness, but according to his own mercy, by the washing
of regeneration and renewal of the Holy Spirit, whom he
poured out on us richly through Jesus Christ our Savior.
TITUS 3:4–6 ESV

Most people have a narrow self-focus on their own affairs and schedules. So when someone goes out of their way to do something nice, they pause at the simple act of a selfless deed and wonder at its root, *Why would you do that for me?*

Jesus saved you by the most shocking act of kindness ever: He was whipped and mocked and spat upon, and His hands and feet were pierced with nails—He died in your place. Now it falls to you to carry on His work. Capture someone today with the kindness of Jesus. Lock them in the magnetic power of His goodness. They will gravitate to His grace and be transformed by His truth.

Lord, lead me to the acts of kindness You
have planned for me today. Amen.

GOD USES ALL THINGS FOR YOUR GOOD

*The king's heart is like channels of water in the hand
of the LORD; He turns it wherever He wishes.*
PROVERBS 21:1 NASB

The Israelites, enslaved by the Egyptians, were growing in number. This concerned the king of Egypt. He told the Hebrew midwives to kill any boys that were born. Yet two midwives, who feared God more than Pharaoh, let the boys live!

Thus, the life of Jochebed's baby, Moses, was spared! Jochebed put Moses in a basket and set him amid the reeds of the Nile. When Pharaoh's daughter came down to bathe, she saw Moses and pitied him. The princess raised Moses in her home, where he was well provided for and well educated (see Exodus 1–2).

God directs people and situations to work for your good no matter how evil or dire they appear to be. God can turn all things to whatever end He pleases!

*Knowing You turn what seems evil and dire to
Your own amazing ends gives me such peace and
comfort! All praise and glory to my Lord!*

COURAGE TO SPEAK

*"For if you keep silent at this time, relief and deliverance
will rise for the Jews from another place, but you and your
father's house will perish. And who knows whether you
have not come to the kingdom for such a time as this?"*
ESTHER 4:14 ESV

Have you ever watched a wrong play out in front of you but done
nothing to right it or prevent it from happening? Or maybe you
did say something but were then criticized or ostracized from the
group. God has strategically positioned you in your exact life. Just
as Esther had to choose whether she would stand up or shut up,
so do we. Whether it's the hurtful injustice of sharing gossip or
the mass tragedy of countless abortions, how do you know that
you weren't put in your corner of earth for such a time as this?
Will you remain silent?

*Heavenly Father, give me wisdom and courage to speak
the truth—but always tempered by love. Amen.*

GOD IS NEAR THE CRUSHED AND BROKENHEARTED

The LORD hears his people when they call to him for help.
He rescues them from all their troubles. The LORD is close to
the brokenhearted; he rescues those whose spirits are crushed.
PSALM 34:17–18 NLT

When crushed and brokenhearted, you may find it hard to see through the tears or speak through the sobs. But that's just what you need to do, for God has His eye upon you. He sees what has happened. He longs to give you comfort, courage, and strength. He wants to hold you, to pour His love and attention upon you, to stroke your soul and raise your spirit.

When you are at the lowest of lows, cry out to God for help. Tell Him all about it. He will hear your voice from heaven and respond. God will rescue you from all your troubles. He will draw so close that you won't know where you end and He begins. Here, the healing will begin.

It is so good to know that I can come to You and cry upon
Your shoulder, Lord. That You have your eye upon me and are
looking to help and heal me. May Yours be the first comfort
I seek when my heart is breaking and my spirit crushed.

GENEROUS IN EVERY WAY

*God can pour on the blessings in astonishing ways so that you're
ready for anything and everything, more than just ready to do
what needs to be done. As one psalmist puts it, He throws caution
to the winds, giving to the needy in reckless abandon. His right-
living, right-giving ways never run out, never wear out. This most
generous God who gives seed to the farmer that becomes bread
for your meals is more than extravagant with you. He gives you
something you can then give away, which grows into full-formed
lives, robust in God, wealthy in every way, so that you can be
generous in every way, producing with us great praise to God.*

2 Corinthians 9:8–11 msg

Mine. Mine. Mine. Sadly it's a mantra that's heard not just in
preschool classrooms. Do you tend to think of the blessings God
gives you as yours? Instead of tightly holding your gifts from God,
try resting those blessings on open palms.

Generally, we're sharers or hoarders. Do you give freely of
what you have? It might be spending time to help a friend (or a
stranger!) or to really listen to what others say when they speak.
Or it could be money, food, a skill that you have, spiritual wisdom
you've gained, clothes you don't wear (or even some you do!).
God is extravagant with you! Pay it forward, and profit great
praise to God!

*Father, may Your freehanded blessings
pass through me to others. Amen.*

GOD VIES FOR YOUR ATTENTION

*Moses said, I will now turn aside and see this great sight,
why the bush is not burned. And when the Lord saw that he
turned aside to see, God called to him out of the midst of the
bush and said, Moses, Moses! And he said, Here am I.*
EXODUS 3:3–4 AMPC

After being raised by Pharaoh's daughter, killing an Egyptian, and
fleeing to escape Pharaoh's wrath, Moses became a shepherd in
Midian. There he married a priest's daughter and became a father.

Forty years later, Pharaoh died, and Moses was still shep-
herding his father-in-law's flock, walking a track he'd been down
many times before. That's when the Angel of the Lord appeared
as a flame in the middle of a bush, yet the bush wasn't destroyed.
Moses turned aside to see this unusual sight. And when God saw
him turn, He spoke.

Just as God wanted Moses' attention, He wants yours. He
wants to reveal His purpose and path for you. But if you rush by,
you'll miss Him. So slow down and keep your eyes open.

*I don't want to miss Your message, Lord. So I'm slowing
down. My eyes and ears are open. Speak, Lord. Here I am!*

Day 240

DOERS

Be doers of the word, and not hearers only, deceiving yourselves.
For if anyone is a hearer of the word and not a doer, he is like
a man who looks intently at his natural face in a mirror.
For he looks at himself and goes away and at once forgets
what he was like. But the one who looks into the perfect
law, the law of liberty, and perseveres, being no hearer who
forgets but a doer who acts, he will be blessed in his doing.

JAMES 1:22–25 ESV

We all have bad days, ones where our peachy attitudes take a sour turn. But don't allow that phase to become your lifestyle. Integrity is doing what we know is right, even when no one is watching. Is your integrity intact?

We can't hide even our secret thoughts from God. He knows all our motives, attitudes, and actions. God sees the real you and loves you still. In fact, He loves you too much to leave you where you are! That's why He's working to make you more like Jesus.

Lord, make me into the daughter You desire. Help me be a
doer of Your Word even when no one else is looking. Amen.

GOD SHAPES AND RESHAPES YOU

All those people who didn't seem interested in what God
was doing actually embraced what God was doing as he
straightened out their lives. And Israel, who seemed so
interested in reading and talking about what God was doing,
missed it. . . . Because instead of trusting God, they took over.
They were absorbed in what they themselves were doing.
ROMANS 9:30–32 MSG

God is the Potter; you're the lump of clay on His wheel (see Isaiah 64:8). You're to be pliant, willing to allow God to shape and reshape you. That means spending time with God and His Word. It means embracing what God's doing in your life and walking where He wills.

Although you want to serve God, there's danger in becoming like the people of Israel, who tried to get right with God by following the law and traditions. "They were so absorbed in their 'God projects' that they didn't notice God right in front of them" (Romans 9:32 MSG).

Be willing to let God shape and reshape you as He lovingly molds you into the awesome woman He created you to be.

Lord, I want to be a woman after Your own heart. So I put myself
upon Your wheel. Lovingly shape me, Lord, as You see fit!

Day 242
CLEAN UP MY HEART

Create in me a clean heart, O God,
and renew a right spirit within me.
PSALM 51:10 ESV

Thankfully God is not wearied by the daily housekeeping chore of shining up our hearts. He never tires of setting things right in our spirits. When poor attitudes, selfishness, or unforgiveness stomp muddy prints through the halls of our freshly washed hearts, He's ready to scrub the mess with a mop sprinkled in conviction and grace.

Day after day we try to keep our lives pure, but each day we end up soiled in some puddle of sin. We can't make our hearts pristine, but He can!

Thank You, God, that You are steadfast in Your love for
me. May my love for You be just as unwavering. Amen.

Day 243

GOD GIVES YOU TALENTS

"His master replied, 'Well done, good and faithful servant! You have been faithful with a few things; I will put you in charge of many things. Come and share your master's happiness!... For whoever has will be given more, and they will have an abundance.'"
MATTHEW 25:21, 29 NIV

Jesus tells a parable about a man who was going on a journey. Before leaving, he entrusted his gold to three servants. To the first, he gave five bags, to the second, two, and to the third, one. When he returned, he learned that the first man with five talents had earned five more. His master commended him, as he did the second man, who began with two bags and earned two more. He reprimanded the third man who, in fear, hid his one bag of gold.

God has gifted you certain abilities and talents. Use them as you follow Him. When you do, He'll give you even more to share for His glory!

Speak into my heart, Lord. Reveal the abilities and talents You want me to use to serve You and help others. Then give me the courage to use them for Your kingdom and glory.

Day 244

BRING PEACE

*Walk in a manner worthy of the calling to which you
have been called, with all humility and gentleness,
with patience, bearing with one another in love, eager to
maintain the unity of the Spirit in the bond of peace.*
EPHESIANS 4:1–3 ESV

People are a messy business. Jesus knew this well. He dealt with His share of hypocrites, angry criticism, and injustice. Yet He came to this world to offer us peace—the peace of God that surpasses all understanding, the peace of forgiveness, grace, and new life, not anger and judgment. The Son of God calls us into our inheritance as children of God by following in His steps as peacemakers. When you're tempted to react in anger, remember whose child you are. Meet discord with the humility, gentleness, patience, and the love of Christ.

*Heavenly Father, help me to bring peace in
gentleness and not an angry response. Amen.*

Day 245

GOD FEEDS AND CLOTHES YOU

"Why worry about your clothing? Look at the lilies of the field and how they grow. They don't work or make their clothing, yet Solomon in all his glory was not dressed as beautifully as they are."
MATTHEW 6:28–29 NLT

Have no doubt God will feed and clothe you who are so much more valuable to Him than sparrows or flowers. Worrying doesn't add one bit of value to your life. On the contrary, it sucks all the joy out of it.

When you feel anxious, go to God. His love has no limits. It will refresh you like the dew from heaven, making you blossom and sending your roots deep into the soil of His Word (see Hosea 14:4–5), proof of how much He cares for you.

Lord, help me to always remember how much You love, care for, and value me. That You'll see I have all I need and more. I want to live worry-free, knowing Your hand is always overflowing in goodness and provision for me.

FORGIVE

"Whenever you stand praying, forgive, if you have anything against anyone, so that your Father also who is in heaven may forgive you your trespasses."
MARK 11:25 ESV

Maybe you've been abandoned or hurt by those who were supposed to love you. That kind of pain can leave you leery of trusting again. Anger and bitterness can find purchase in your torn-up soul. But there is hope. Forgiveness is possible. Someone else was betrayed by friends, whipped, and beaten. His body was pierced by nails, and He gave up His life for you. In the midst of His anguished body and soul, He cried out, "Father, forgive them" (Luke 23:34 ESV).

And He also forgives you. In Christ we can forgive much because we have been forgiven everything. Rest your weary mind. His righteous judgment will come in His time. His justice will reign. Forgive, and find peace.

Lord, bring true forgiveness and healing to my heart. Amen.

GOD IS EAGER FOR YOUR TRUST AND LISTENING EAR

"If you will give earnest heed to the voice of the LORD your God, and do what is right in His sight, and give ear to His commandments, and keep all His statutes, I will put none of the diseases on you which I have put on the Egyptians; for I, the LORD, am your healer."
EXODUS 15:26 NASB

The Israelites, thirsting for lack of water, reached Marah. But, it's waters being bitter, the people complained to Moses. After Moses cried out to God, God showed Moses a stick and told him to throw it into the water. Moses did, and the water became sweet enough to drink. That's when God told them, "If you listen to Me, I won't plague but heal you."

Only God knows the truth of your circumstances. He's seen what's going to happen next. So instead of rolling out a list of your complaints, stop. Trust God. Open your ears to what He wants you to do, and He'll lead you to abundant water (see Exodus 15:27).

Help me, Lord, to trust and keep my eyes on You, not my circumstances.

THROUGH HIS EYES

*"You are precious in my eyes,
and honored, and I love you."*
ISAIAH 43:4 ESV

God sees the same word etched across the broken surface of every life—*precious*. Each and every one matters to Him. He suffers with the pain of their heartaches. He cares about the burdens they stumble beneath. He longs for their presence in His kingdom. He treasures their soul with the same tenderness He gives to yours.

Circumstances in this world may have been more kind to you than others—or maybe not. Whether this world deems you as valuable or worthless, your Father in heaven has better names for you: precious, unique, beloved, worthy, forgiven, pure. He calls you daughter.

*Heavenly Father, give me fresh eyes. Give me Your eyes
so I can see others as You do. In Jesus' name, amen.*

GOD PROTECTS YOU WHERE HE DIRECTS YOU

He arose and rebuked the wind and said to the sea,
Hush now! Be still (muzzled)! And the wind ceased
(sank to rest as if exhausted by its beating) and there
was [immediately] a great calm (a perfect peacefulness).
MARK 4:39 AMPC

After preaching all day to a large crowd, Jesus directed the disciples to cross to the other side of the lake. So they started rowing as Jesus fell asleep in the back of the boat. But a terrible storm came up. The high waves were crashing, pouring into the boat, filling it with water. The disciples panicked (Mark 4:38).

Jesus got up and rebuked the wind, and suddenly it stopped and there was a wonderful calm. Then He said to the disciples, "Why are you so timid and fearful? How is it that you have no faith (no firmly relying trust)?" (Mark 4:40 AMPC).

When storms assail you, turn to Jesus with the assurance that He is in your boat and will protect you wherever He's directed you to go.

Jesus, thank You for riding through good days and bad with
me. I trust You to see me safely through all my crossings!

CONQUEROR

"Behold, I have given you authority to tread on serpents and scorpions, and over all the power of the enemy, and nothing shall hurt you."
Luke 10:19 esv

As a child of God, you have an enemy in this world whose traps for you aren't innocently or carelessly left behind. He has been studying human nature for a very long time, and he has an arsenal of tricks to draw you away from God. He wants to take you out—out of peace, out of freedom, out of God's plans, and out of life everlasting.

But don't fear, brave friend. Satan is predictable. He's a liar. You can combat his lies with God's truth. Study scripture. Memorize it. Learn Satan's strategy so you won't be caught in his snares. And know this: "We are more than conquerors through him who loved us" (Romans 8:37 esv).

Lord, give me wisdom to avoid Satan's traps. Amen.

Day 251

GOD GIVES YOU
CREATIVE POWER

*Do not neglect the gift which is in you. . .which was directly
imparted to you [by the Holy Spirit]. . . . Practice and cultivate and
meditate upon these duties; throw yourself wholly into them [as
your ministry], so that your progress may be evident to everybody.*
1 TIMOTHY 4:14–15 AMPC

Because you were made in God's image (see Genesis 1:27), you
have been endowed with creative abilities. And when you accepted Jesus, the Holy Spirit gave you special spiritual gifts.
Those gifts may be teaching, preaching, writing, encouraging,
singing, painting, organizing, hospitality. . .you name it! All to
help extend and build up God's kingdom.

Don't neglect that special gift that only you can use to
help others. Find out what it is then throw yourself into using
your particular ability, making it a ministry that will make this
world a better place—and give you joy as you serve your Master
Creator.

*Thank You, Lord, for giving me creative power. Lead me to what
that gift is and how I can hone it. Then show me how You would
like me to use it for Your kingdom and glory—and my joy!*

Day 252

PAUSE TO LISTEN

"My sheep listen to my voice;
I know them, and they follow me."
JOHN 10:27 NIV

How intently do we listen for God's voice during our day or even during our quiet time? Slowing the raging river of our thoughts feels like an impossible task at times. But how are we to participate in God's plans for our day if we don't stop to hear His words?

Try a new prayer strategy today—listen more and talk less. God does care about all your needs and problems, but often our prayers devolve into a lengthy laundry list of wants and worries. The Creator of the universe, the mighty God of heaven, has plans for you today. Pause the patter of your spilling words and wait. Be still. Listen. Welcome His input into your conversation.

Lord, teach me to listen for Your voice
in the moments of my day. Amen.

GOD MADE A BRAND-NEW YOU

*Therefore if any person is [ingrafted] in Christ (the
Messiah) he is a new creation (a new creature altogether);
the old [previous moral and spiritual condition] has
passed away. Behold, the fresh and new has come!*
2 CORINTHIANS 5:17 AMPC

Jesus has saved you! You are now washed of sins, are living an eternal life, and participate in Christ's divine nature. The old you—who you were *before* you knew and accepted Christ—is now gone. Your old beliefs, fears, plans, loves, value system, and priorities are gone. You see things a new way—through Christ's eyes. And the Holy Spirit is on hand to help direct, steer, comfort, inspire, and prompt you to live in and for Christ, following His direction, lead, and path.

God made you a brand-new person, one who treasures the things of heaven instead of the things of the earth. Praise God for your new start in this eternal life!

I am so happy that You have saved me, Jesus. That I have the Spirit to help me. That because of You, God sees me as a new creature, holy and perfect. Help me live this life Your way.

COME CLOSER

Since we have confidence to enter the holy places by the blood of Jesus, by the new and living way that he opened for us through the curtain, that is, through his flesh, and since we have a great priest over the house of God, let us draw near with a true heart in full assurance of faith, with our hearts sprinkled clean from an evil conscience and our bodies washed with pure water. Let us hold fast the confession of our hope without wavering, for he who promised is faithful.
HEBREWS 10:19–23 ESV

The sunshine pulls you. It woos you outside into its warm embrace. You close your eyes and tilt your face up to receive its gentle kiss on your skin. A smile touches your lips, and your worries seem to melt away.

Jesus is the brilliant, shining sun to this dark and troubled world. His love is magnetic. And through Him we find hope. Hope for our future. Hope for our present. Hope for our families. Hope for our problems. Hope through our failures.

Step out of the cold shadows and into His light. Energize your tired and chilly soul in the sunshine of His promises. Come in from the cold. You don't have to do this life alone.

Jesus, draw me closer. I'm holding on tight to my hope in You because You are faithful. Amen.

Day 255

GOD GIVES YOU DISCERNMENT

Don't let anyone divert you from the truth. It's the person
who acts right who is right, just as we see it lived out in our
righteous Messiah. Those who make a practice of sin are
straight from the Devil, the pioneer in the practice of sin.
The Son of God entered the scene to abolish the Devil's ways.
1 JOHN 3:7–8 MSG

Sometimes it's hard to tell who the "good guys" are in this world. But through the apostle John, God gives you guidance in this area so you won't be led astray by people who aren't living the "right" (righteous) way. Although some people seem to talk a good game, if they're not practicing what they teach but are habitually sinning, they're not walking in the light.

The "good guys" are the ones living the right way, following Jesus' example. They truly reflect Jesus' light. The good guys are the ones whose example you'll want to emulate as God continues to build up your faith and life in Christ.

Thank You, Lord, for giving me a
litmus test so I won't be led astray!

ALL-POWERFUL JESUS

*"I lay down my life that I may take it up again. No one takes it
from me, but I lay it down of my own accord. I have authority
to lay it down, and I have authority to take it up again."*
JOHN 10:17–18 ESV

Jesus has ultimate authority. In heaven and in earth, Jesus can
make things happen. He's no frail Savior. Don't get the wrong
idea that just because He was nailed to a cross that His power
and authority were ever in question. No, those soldiers didn't
kill Jesus on that cross. The Lord of the universe laid down His
life—willingly. For me. For you.

This is the same Jesus who stilled a violent storm with a few
words. The same Jesus who commanded demons. This Jesus had
authority both to lay down His life and to pick it back up again
three days later and walk out of a tomb. This is your Jesus too!

*Heavenly Father, thank You for the resurrection—
the evidence that You have all the power! In Jesus' name, amen.*

GOD VALUES AND BLESSES YOUR SERVANT'S HEART

"If I then, the Lord and the Teacher, washed your feet,
you also ought to wash one another's feet. For I gave you
an example that you also should do as I did to you. . . .
If you know these things, you are blessed if you do them."
JOHN 13:14–15, 17 NASB

Imagine living in a society where, before you sat down for a meal, good hosts made sure a non-Jewish slave washed your feet, dusty from your travels on the road. Now imagine being Jesus' disciple. You're in the middle of dinner and the Son of God gets up, takes off His coat, ties a towel around His waist, pours water in a basin, and begins to wash your dirty, stinky feet!

How astounding, unusual, against the norm—but that was Jesus!

Be like Jesus. Be humble and have a servant's heart, not judging who you should minister to. If you do these things, God will bless you.

Show me, Lord, who I can humbly serve as I walk Your way today.

Day 258
BEAUTIFUL ONE

The Mighty One, God the Lord, speaks and summons the earth
from the rising of the sun to its setting. Out of Zion, the perfection of
beauty, God shines forth. Our God comes; he does not keep silence;
before him is a devouring fire, around him a mighty tempest.
Psalm 50:1–3 esv

God's work brings forth beauty not only around us but in us as well. His nature is beauty, so He cannot help but birth more beauty around Him and in those in which His very Spirit dwells. He desires the imperishable beauty of a gentle and quiet spirit in us. May your life be infused with grace, gentleness, and peace. May you be an image-bearer of His beauty today.

Father, we can't look on Your glory. And the brilliance of a
sunset is only a vague reflection of Your glorious beauty.
May I bear the image of even a small portion of Your love,
Your grace, and Your beautiful Spirit today. Amen.

GOD HELPS YOU UNDERSTAND

*"But there is a spirit within people, the breath of the
Almighty within them, that makes them intelligent."*
JOB 32:8 NLT

When God created humankind, He breathed the breath of life
into them (see Genesis 2:7). That breath gave them not only a
life force but also intelligence.

Jesus breathed the Holy Spirit onto the disciples, who were
hiding in the upper room after His resurrection (see John 20:22).
He did that to give them a taste of what they'd receive when the
Holy Spirit would be given to live within them at Pentecost.

As a believer, you have the breath of God within you. You've
been given wisdom from above in the form of the Holy Spirit.

Got a problem? Can't understand something? Go to God. He
has all the wisdom, intelligence, and knowledge you need—and
so much more.

*Thank You, Lord, for giving me wisdom when
I'm stymied, confused, or uncertain of which way
to go, what to do. With Your breath upon me and
Your Spirit within me, I know I'll find my way.*

ALIVE IN HIM

*You also must consider yourselves dead
to sin and alive to God in Christ Jesus.*
ROMANS 6:11 ESV

Our sight sometimes gets hung up on "dead" things. We forget what God has said and return to old sins and habits that lead only to death, just as the women visiting Jesus' tomb did not remember that Jesus said He would rise. But Jesus has delivered us from death into new life. He has taken the punishment of hell for us and conquered death. He came through it and stepped out of the tomb alive! Drop your old dead things and embrace godly habits that lead to life. Live like you are alive in Him!

*Jesus, You delivered me from death. You satisfied
heaven's justice for me. Help me live for You. Amen.*

GOD WORKS MIRACLES IN YOUR LIFE

This, the first of His signs (miracles, wonderworks),
Jesus performed in Cana of Galilee, and manifested His glory
[by it He displayed His greatness and His power openly], and His
disciples believed in Him [adhered to, trusted in, and relied on Him].
JOHN 2:11 AMPC

Through people and other tools, God worked many miracles in the Old and New Testaments. He parted waters, healed lepers, supplied an abundance of oil for a poor widow, crumbled walls at the sound of trumpets and shouts, brought water gushing out of a rock. . . He also chased out demons, calmed the wind, smoothed over the sea, turned water into wine, raised the dead . . . Later, Jesus' followers performed many miracles in His name!

When you need a miracle, pray for God's help. Put yourself and your situation in Jesus' hands, and open your eyes of faith so you will see His "sign" when it comes—proof of His eternal, miracle-working power!

Lord, I am putting myself and my circumstances in
Your worthy hands. Work Your miracle, Lord, and give
me the eyes of faith so I can see it and praise You!

Day 262

KINDNESS IS COOL

*"I tell you, love your enemies. Help and give without
expecting a return. You'll never—I promise—regret it.
Live out this God-created identity the way our Father
lives toward us, generously and graciously, even when
we're at our worst. Our Father is kind; you be kind."*
LUKE 6:35–36 MSG

That's it! The perfect comeback. The zinger you've been rehearsing
in your head for a week is now poised on the tip of your tongue.
You're already anticipating your smug satisfaction in knowing
you let this woman have what she deserved.

But will you feel satisfied? Most likely instead of feeling
gratified, you'll spend the remainder of your week wishing for
the chance to snatch back that moment and curb your tongue.

Wouldn't it be better to be kind? Kindness definitely comes
with less cringe-worthy strings attached! Serve out an extra
measure of grace and kindness when you encounter hostility
and crankiness—just like Jesus does for you.

*Lord, guard my words. My demeanor and behavior are
a reflection of the one I belong to—You, Jesus. Amen.*

GOD EMPATHIZES WITH YOU

*In all their affliction He was afflicted, and the
Angel of His presence saved them; in His love
and in His pity He redeemed them; and He lifted
them up and carried them all the days of old.*
ISAIAH 63:9 AMPC

Jesus never once stopped following God's will for His life. Even though He was homeless, with no place to lay His head, He never once deviated from God's path. The night before He died, Jesus "began to show grief and distress of mind and was deeply depressed" (Matthew 26:37 AMPC). And still He prayed, "Nevertheless, not what I will [not what I desire], but as You will and desire" (Matthew 26:39 AMPC).

Jesus knows what you're going through. He and the angel of His presence have saved you because He loves and pities you. He has compassion for you. So, when the going gets tough, go to Jesus. Allow Him to lift you up and carry you His way.

*Lift me up, Lord. Carry me to the peace
of Your presence as I live Your way.*

FEAR NOT!

*"Are not two sparrows sold for a penny? And not one of
them will fall to the ground apart from your Father."*
MATTHEW 10:29 ESV

Horrible things sometimes happen, and evil does exist. But Jesus
offers hope. He confronted the darkness of this world and said,
"Do not fear those who kill the body but cannot kill the soul.
Rather fear him who can destroy both soul and body in hell"
(Matthew 10:28 ESV). In other words, Jesus says, "The only one
you should be afraid of is Me."

Jesus holds all the cards. The power of eternal life is in His
hands. Do you know Him? Do you call Him friend? Can you rest
today in the peace of His promise?

*Jesus, thank You that I don't have to fear even death
because my eternal future is secure in You. Amen.*

GOD CALLS YOU A CHILD OF THE MOST HIGH

"But love your enemies, do good to them, and lend to them
without expecting to get anything back. Then your reward
will be great, and you will be children of the Most High,
because he is kind to the ungrateful and wicked."

LUKE 6:35 NIV

Jesus loved turning the world on its ears! In Matthew 5:43 (NIV), He reminded the people that they'd heard it said that they should "Love your neighbor," a quote from the law of Moses (see Leviticus 19:18). But to that He added the scribes' and Pharisees' interpretation and application of that command: "and hate your enemy."

Fortunately, Jesus came to clarify lots of things, including the idea that you're *not* to hate your enemies but *love* them! And, time and time again, God is kind to those who are not just unthankful but evil. So, like Father, like daughter!

Today show God that you value Him as much as He values you, by loving an enemy. Doing so comes with a wonderful reward!

Lord of all, show me how to bless and love my enemies.
Then give me the means to do so—for You!

Day 266

MY JESUS

*His eyes were like a flame of fire, his feet were like
burnished bronze, refined in a furnace, and his
voice was like the roar of many waters.*
REVELATION 1:14–15 ESV

Consider the great, wonderful, amazing, and awe-inducing power of the living God of the universe. Spend some time contemplating just what God is capable of. Because if you don't know the power of God, then you will be afraid of what life may throw at you. You will fear death, illness, the future, or what's going to happen to your kids. Don't live a life of fear. Read the opening chapter of Revelation and see Jesus unmasked. He's no fuzzy bunny, my friend. But He is still your Jesus.

What kind of Jesus are you serving? Is He timid and fluffy or powerful and frightening to His enemies?

*Jesus, You are the mighty one who walked through
death for me and came out alive. Wipe away my
fears of this life as I live in Your power. Amen.*

GOD SENDS MESSENGERS TO KEEP YOU SAFE

An angel of the Lord appeared to Joseph in a dream.
"Get up! Flee to Egypt with the child and his mother,"
the angel said. "Stay there until I tell you to return."
MATTHEW 2:13 NLT

For Joseph, messages came from a dream angel. The first told him not to send away but to marry his wife-to-be, an already-pregnant Mary (see Matthew 1:19–24). Later, wise men visiting Jesus were warned by a dream angel not to stop at Herod's place and tell him where they'd found the Boy-King (see Matthew 2:12). When the wise men left, Joseph was warned by a dream angel to take Jesus to Egypt so Herod wouldn't kill Him (see Matthew 2:13). Later a dream angel told Joseph that those seeking to kill Jesus had died and it was now safe to go back to Israel (see Matthew 2:19–21).

When you get a warning from God or one of His personal messengers, heed it. He'll keep you safe.

Lord, I want to play it safe. Open my
ears and eyes to hear Your messages.

WHEN MOUNTAINS CRUMBLE

*God is our refuge and strength, always ready to help in times
of trouble. So we will not fear when earthquakes come and
the mountains crumble into the sea. . . . The LORD of Heaven's
Armies is here among us; the God of Israel is our fortress.*
PSALM 46:1–2, 7 NLT

Sometimes our emotions bushwhack us. They build until the
rising pressure forces an eruption of volcanic proportions. We
spew destruction, often hurting the ones we love best. But God
has promised to be our refuge through much bigger problems
than a dirty sink. He promises to be your refuge even if the
mountains fall into the sea. Today, ask God to take your struggle
with anger and fear and use it to bring new life and strength
instead of destruction.

*Father, help me sort out my raw emotions.
Show me how to take baby steps into new life. Amen.*

GOD GIVES YOU JESUS— YOUR MANNA FOR LIFE

"Your ancestors ate manna in the wilderness, but they all died. Anyone who eats the bread from heaven, however, will never die. I am the living bread that came down from heaven. Anyone who eats this bread will live forever; and this bread, which I will offer. . .is my flesh."
JOHN 6:49–51 NLT

When the Israelites began their wilderness wandering, they began to hunger. They complained to Moses. So God rained down bread from heaven, something the Israelites had never seen before. They called it *manna,* meaning, "What is it?" (Exodus 16:15 NLT). Yet this manna was temporary, a small foreshadowing of what Jesus would provide.

When Jesus came, He said *He* was the bread God gave from heaven and that all who ate this bread would never die! Jesus offered His body, His flesh, on the cross so you could live forever. With Jesus, the Bread of Life, you have all the nourishment you'll ever need. All you require comes from and is found in Him—your manna for life!

Thank You, God, for giving me all I need to live—in Jesus!

BREAD OF LIFE

*"It is written, 'Man shall not live by bread alone,
but by every word that comes from the mouth of God.' "*
<small>MATTHEW 4:4 ESV</small>

Jesus had been fasting in the wilderness for forty days. He had to be getting desperately hungry. Satan zeroed in on Jesus' weak spot and mocked Him—if He was the Son of God, He should just turn some stones into bread.

Jesus said something like, "Do you think that mere bread can sustain your life? Live on a steady diet of the words from God's mouth."

Jesus says eat bread and live for a day. Eat the Word of God, chew on it, internalize it until it becomes enmeshed in the fiber of your being—and you will *truly* live. Not just for today, but forever!

God, may I read Your words—and live! Amen.

GOD GOES THE DISTANCE FOR YOU

*The king's officer pleaded with Him, Sir, do come down
at once before my little child is dead! Jesus answered him,
Go in peace; your son will live! And the man put his
trust in what Jesus said and started home.*

JOHN 4:49–50 AMPC

Jesus was in Cana when a Roman official begged Him to come
with him to Capernaum. It was there, a sixteen-mile journey,
where his son lay dying. Jesus told the officer to go in peace and
that his son would live. Trusting Jesus at His word, the man
started the journey back home. But while he was on his way, his
servants met up with him and told him, "Your son lives!" (John
4:51 AMPC). When the official asked when the boy had begun to
get better, they named the same hour that Jesus had said to him,
"Your son will live" (John 4:53 AMPC).

There is no distance God will not cover to answer your prayer
when you trust in Him for the results.

*You've proven time and time again, Lord, that You will go the
distance for me when I ask You for help and take You at Your word.
Today, I go in peace, knowing You hear and will answer my prayer!*

Day 272

MOVING UP

*"He will wipe away every tear from their eyes, and death
shall be no more, neither shall there be mourning, nor crying,
nor pain anymore, for the former things have passed away."*
REVELATION 21:4 ESV

When the burdens of this life threaten to break you, remember that this world is not your forever home. Life here has its patched plaster and foundation cracks. But don't despair in your current circumstances. Jesus knows how hard this life can hit. He was beaten up by it too.

But this is not the end of your house hunt. Jesus is right now with the Father, getting your new place ready for you. And none of the things that trouble us here will follow us there. The Creator is designing a home for you. It's exciting. It's custom built. Just wait and see! . . . It's going to be jaw-dropping.

*Lord, no more tears, no more pain or sins,
no more death to worry about. I can hardly
imagine how wonderful it will be with You! Amen.*

Day 273

GOD IS YOUR FOREVER COMPANION

The people said, "You aren't even fifty years old. How can you say you have seen Abraham?" Jesus answered, "I tell you the truth, before Abraham was even born, I AM."
JOHN 8:57–58 NLT

When God appeared to Moses in the burning bush, Moses asked Him what His name was. That's when God told Moses, "I AM WHO I AM. Say this to the people of Israel: I AM has sent me to you" (Exodus 3:14 NLT).

Now here is Jesus, thousands of years later, telling people that *He* is the I AM, the eternal one, that He was around before Abraham was even born! That means God and Jesus always have been, always are, and always will be. They are your forever companions, there to aid, love, provide for, and give you hope wherever and whenever you need them—all the years of your life and beyond!

It's hard to grasp how eternal You are, Lord. But I'm so grateful for Your forever presence as we walk this road together!

LESSON IN SERVICE

"He who is least among you all is the one who is great."
LUKE 9:48 ESV

When Jesus and the disciples sat down for the Passover meal, no one offered to scrub feet. So Jesus took off His shirt, grabbed a towel and a basin, and began to wash the dirt from their feet. Jesus. The Son of God. The Creator of the universe. The Alpha and Omega. He knelt and took up the job of the lowest servant. The disciples must have cringed, thinking, *I should be the one doing this! Not Jesus*. But Jesus then said they were to follow His example.

Our communities and our churches should be better because we are in them. Roll up your sleeves and ask, "How can I help?"

Jesus, teach me to have a humble heart.
Teach me to serve. Amen.

GOD GIVES YOU COURAGE— JUST WHEN YOU NEED IT

Joseph, he of Arimathea, noble and honorable in rank and a
respected member of the council (Sanhedrin), who was himself
waiting for the kingdom of God, daring the consequences, took
courage and ventured to go to Pilate and asked for the body of Jesus.
MARK 15:43 AMPC

Joseph of Arimathea was a rich and respected Jewish leader. He was also one of the few who hadn't agreed with the decisions and actions of the other religious leaders (see Luke 23:51). In fact, Joseph had been a disciple of Jesus, but he kept that secret because he feared the Jews (see John 19:38).

Yet God gave Joseph the courage to ask Pilate for permission to take down Jesus' body, then he wrapped it with spices and placed it in a new tomb carved out of rock.

God gives those He loves and values the courage to do what He prompts them to do—regardless of the consequences. You too will be given the same courage!

You know the things I'm afraid to do, Lord. Give me
the courage, just as You did Joseph, to dare to do what
You're calling me to do, in Jesus' name. Amen.

BE KNOWN BY YOUR LOVE

*Suppose a brother or a sister is without clothes and daily food.
If one of you says to them, "Go in peace; keep warm and well fed,"
but does nothing about their physical needs, what good is it? In the
same way, faith by itself, if it is not accompanied by action, is dead.*
JAMES 2:15–17 NIV

How can we measure our devotion to Jesus? Is it the number of times we attend church services on any given week? The amount of money we place into the offering plate? By tattooing the object of our affection right on our skin? . . .

Please understand: the mark of Jesus is not a tattoo. But He did tell His disciples exactly what His mark on their lives would look like: "All people will know that you are my disciples, if you have love for one another" (John 13:35 ESV).

Jesus cared about people. He reached out to them with healing and forgiveness and compassion. He loved them. Does your love for the struggling people of this world mark you as His?

*Heavenly Father, I want to be known as Yours.
Place Your mark of love upon my life. Amen.*

Day 277

GOD REALIGNS YOUR VALUES

*"Don't store up treasures here on earth, where moths eat them
and rust destroys them, and where thieves break in and steal.
Store your treasures in heaven, where moths and rust cannot
destroy, and thieves do not break in and steal. Wherever your
treasure is, there the desires of your heart will also be."*
MATTHEW 6:19–21, 24 NLT

Jesus presents you with a choice. You can either be focused on
the things of this earth or—and it's a big "OR"—you can be focused
on the things of heaven. It's a choice between having your heart
set on living for and loving creation or living for and loving the
Creator.

When you follow Jesus, God helps you realign your values.
He urges you to trust, serve, and rely on Him alone. He asks
that you place your focus and desire on valuing and treasuring
Him and His will only, realizing He alone is sufficient for all
you need or want. He wants the best path for you.

*Lord, help me reevaluate what I think is important
in this life. Show me where my heart is, and help
me get better aligned with You.*

Day 278

GROWING UP

*Practice these things, immerse yourself in them,
so that all may see your progress.*
1 TIMOTHY 4:15 ESV

Many followers of Jesus are living stunted, disabled spiritual lives because they've grown comfortable with their developmental stage. Paul told the Corinthians he had to address them as infants in Christ and feed them milk because they weren't ready for the meat of God's Word. In Hebrews we're encouraged to "leave the elementary doctrine of Christ and go on to maturity" (Hebrews 6:1 ESV).

Beloved, don't continue crawling when you were meant to run. Cultivate a hunger for the deep things of God. Follow the leading of the Holy Spirit. Study His Word. Learn His ways. You don't want to miss out on the fullness of His breathtaking plans!

Father, teach me something new about You today. Amen.

GOD KEEPS YOU FROM STUMBLING IN THE DARK

*Then Jesus again spoke to them, saying, "I am the
Light of the world; he who follows Me will not walk
in the darkness, but will have the Light of life."*
JOHN 8:12 NASB

Jesus is the Light of the World. He's the light the psalmist wrote
about: "Light, space, zest—that's GOD! So, with him on my side
I'm fearless, afraid of no one and nothing" (Psalm 27:1 MSG).
He's the great light that would be seen by the people who live
in darkness, the light that would guide the nations and restore the people of Israel (see Isaiah 9:2; 42:6). He's the light for
the Gentiles, extending God's salvation to the end of the earth
(see Isaiah 49:6).

As a follower of Jesus, you're in the light and are now to walk
as "children of Light" (Ephesians 5:8 AMPC).

Each day look for the light of God. Allow it to shine within
and be a beam upon your path.

*God, thank You for being the light of my life. Shine Your light
within so I can better reflect Your presence in my life.*

Day 280
COME BACK TO HIM

If I say, "Surely the darkness shall cover me, and the light
about me be night," even the darkness is not dark to you;
the night is bright as the day, for darkness is as light with you.
PSALM 139:11–12 ESV

Have you attempted to hide from God like Adam and Eve? Or run from Him like Jonah? It seems we're all prone to repeat the same ridiculous behavior when being disobedient. It's irrational to think we can give God the slip or dodge His all-seeing glance. It's like running from your shadow. You will never escape. He knows exactly where you are and what you are doing there. Yet He calls out as He did in the Garden of Eden: "Where are you?" (Genesis 3:9 ESV)

Will you answer Him today? Will you step back into the light of His forgiveness?

Father, I'm so sorry. I didn't want You to see me,
but You already know. Please forgive me
and help me to live righteously. Amen.

GOD GIVES YOU THE SPIRIT OF LIVING WATER

*"Let anyone who is thirsty come to me and drink.
Whoever believes in me, as Scripture has said, rivers of living
water will flow from within them." By this he meant the Spirit,
whom those who believed in him were later to receive.*

JOHN 7:37–39 NIV

Jesus is the conduit to the rivers of living water. Those who followed Him received a Helper that came after Jesus went back to heaven so that they would not be left alone. And it's this Helper, the Holy Spirit, who's the living water you now have within you.

In Isaiah 55:1 (NIV), Isaiah wrote, "Come, all you who are thirsty, come to the waters; and you who have no money, come, buy and eat! Come. . .without money and without cost." Jesus is inviting you to freely partake of what your soul needs and craves—He who is the Rock that gushes out water for the thirsty walking in a dry and weary land.

*Lord, I'm thirsting for the comfort and free-flowing
blessings from the Spirit within. Nothing else
will satisfy. So I come and drink.*

WHAT'S YOUR STORY?

But God chose what is foolish in the world to shame the wise;
God chose what is weak in the world to shame the strong;
God chose what is low and despised in the world, even things
that are not, to bring to nothing things that are, so that
no human being might boast in the presence of God.
1 CORINTHIANS 1:27–29 ESV

God isn't a God of waste; He is a God of creativity. Your utter failures, your crushing defeats, your hardships and hurts—He doesn't sweep up the shattered pieces and toss them in a wastebasket. No. He gathers all those precious shards: each jagged corner, every splintered, irregular shape. He spreads them gently before Him and fits them together into something new, something unexpected, something beautiful.

Don't despair if sin has left you fractured and fragile. You are not unusable. You are not garbage. Things that drove you to your knees and broke you can bring you to Jesus. Offer Him your broken life. In the hands of the Master, from what once appeared as nothing more than shattered glass, a stunning mosaic will emerge.

Lord, take my life. Take my story. Use it to
encourage and draw someone to You today. Amen.

Day 283

GOD GAVE YOU THE LORD OF PEACE

Now may the Lord of peace Himself grant you His peace
(the peace of His kingdom) at all times and in all
ways [under all circumstances and conditions,
whatever comes]. The Lord [be] with you all.
2 THESSALONIANS 3:16 AMPC

When Jesus was here on the earth, living the human experience, along with the joy He endured many trials. He was accused of something He didn't do and then was crucified for it. He was beaten, laughed at, mocked, betrayed, abandoned, whipped, and stabbed with a spear. Yet through all of these troubles, He kept the peace of God.

Jesus knows everything you're going through. He's experienced every emotion you're feeling. And He's walking every step of the way with you, for He has promised to never leave or forsake you.

Jesus, I need Your peace each and every day. As I come into
Your presence, shower me with the calm that only You can
provide. Soothe my nerves, give me hope, allow me to rest in
Your arms until I have the peace that is beyond understanding.

Day 284

SLOW DOWN

*My dear brothers and sisters, take note of this: Everyone should
be quick to listen, slow to speak and slow to become angry.*
JAMES 1:19 NIV

"Quick to listen, slow to speak and slow to become angry." This admonition suggests James was well acquainted with the emotional creatures called humans. Surely he arranged his words strategically because he knew that the opposite is usually true. We don't listen. We spew thoughtless words. We misunderstand and we get mad.

What if we listened more carefully? What if your next conversation wasn't about you? What if you chose to believe that the best possible intentions are behind any potentially upsetting comments that come your way? Maybe they were even intended for your good. The next time you hear potentially upsetting comments, take the slow road—slow to overreact, slow to anger. A simple question to clarify their words might just save you a whole lot of stewing in bitter juices.

*Lord, help me weigh my words today before I speak
them. Give me the patience to listen and the wisdom
to choose truth over irrational anger. Amen.*

GOD WANTS YOU TO BREAK THE GOOD NEWS

How beautiful on the mountains are the feet of the messenger
bringing good news, breaking the news that all's well, proclaiming
good times, announcing salvation, telling Zion, "Your God reigns!"
ISAIAH 52:7 MSG

Amazingly enough, the first person to spread the news of Jesus' triumph over death was a woman! When Mary Magdalene went to the tomb looking for Jesus' body, she heard a voice behind her. It was her beloved Jesus saying her name—Mary! She fell down and worshipped Him. But Jesus told her to go and tell the disciples He was going to ascend to Father God. And so she did (see John 20:1–18).

God wants you to tell others about Jesus (see Matthew 28:16–20), what He's done for all people, and what He's done for you. When you do, you too will have beautiful feet!

I am honored that You want to use me to spread the good news,
Lord. Give me the right words to say to others at the right time.
And as I do so, may I be as thrilled as Mary at the tomb.

EXPERIENCE GOD'S FULLNESS

That you, being rooted and grounded in love,
may have strength to comprehend with all the saints
what is the breadth and length and height and depth,
and to know the love of Christ that surpasses knowledge,
that you may be filled with all the fullness of God.
EPHESIANS 3:17–19 ESV

In Ephesians 3, Paul prayed that the believers would begin to understand just how passionately God loves them. His love for us is so cosmically enormous that our minds will never comprehend its dimensions. Are you filled to the measure with the fullness of God, or are you running on empty and searching for something to fill your empty spaces?

When you feel completely enveloped in God's huge love for you, you'll trust Him and fully experience His presence in your life. And because of this you'll be able to love others.

God, fill me with Your fullness so I can love. Amen.

GOD SEEKS THE BEST IN YOU

*Jesus said to him, "Today salvation has come to this
house, because this man, too, is a son of Abraham.
For the Son of Man came to seek and to save the lost."*
LUKE 19:9–10 NIV

Zacchaeus was a despised tax collector. When Jesus was passing
through town, Zacchaeus, short in stature, couldn't see Him, so
he climbed up a sycamore tree.

When Jesus came near Zacchaeus, He looked up and said,
"Zacchaeus, come down immediately. I must stay at your house
today" (Luke 19:5 NIV). The little man shimmied down the tree
and welcomed Jesus to his home. People were less than impressed
that Jesus went to the home of a known sinner (see Luke 19:7
NIV). Zacchaeus told Jesus he would immediately give half his
possessions to the poor and pay back four times the amount he'd
cheated others.

After Jesus enters your heart and you begin to know Him more
intimately, you find yourself willing and able to reform yourself
and your life, doing things you could never do on your own!

*Jesus, thank You for bringing Your light to my life.
Thank You for seeking out and saving me, making me
a better and more joyful servant to, and friend of, You!*

GOD IS FOR YOU

With God on our side like this, how can we lose? If God didn't hesitate to put everything on the line for us, embracing our condition and exposing himself to the worst by sending his own Son, is there anything else he wouldn't gladly and freely do for us? And who would dare tangle with God by messing with one of God's chosen? Who would dare even to point a finger? The One who died for us—who was raised to life for us!—is in the presence of God at this very moment sticking up for us. Do you think anyone is going to be able to drive a wedge between us and Christ's love for us? There is no way! Not trouble, not hard times, not hatred, not hunger, not homelessness, not bullying threats, not backstabbing, not even the worst sins listed in Scripture. . . . None of this fazes us because Jesus loves us. I'm absolutely convinced that nothing—nothing living or dead, angelic or demonic, today or tomorrow, high or low, thinkable or unthinkable—absolutely nothing can get between us and God's love because of the way that Jesus our Master has embraced us.
Romans 8:31–39 msg

Praise Jesus! None of the things that come against us today—not our failures, not our feelings, not even death!—will keep Him from loving us. Live loved today!

God, thank You for Your matchless love. Even death will merely usher me into Your waiting embrace. Amen.

GOD MAKES ALL THINGS CLEAR TO YOU

The woman said to Him, I know that Messiah is coming, He Who is called the Christ (the Anointed One); and when He arrives, He will tell us everything we need to know and make it clear to us. Jesus said to her, I Who now speak with you am He.
JOHN 4:25–26 AMPC

God sent Jesus so you would get to know and understand Him. He wants you to search His Word so that you can find all the blessings He offers.

Allow Jesus to speak to you. Rediscover His parables, and take to heart each one's lesson. Be conscious of the Holy Spirit's translation of God's Word. Trust that He'll point you to the scriptures you personally need to hear. Keep your heart open to God's will and way through prayer and praise. In so doing, you'll better home in on God's purpose for your life.

Rest easy. "For God is not a God of confusion but of peace" (1 Corinthians 14:33 NASB). He'll help you sort things out.

I realize, Lord, that You're the answer to all my questions. And although You won't tell me everything, You'll tell me all I need to know. This alone gives me peace.

Day 290

HE IS ENOUGH

*"Were not the Cushites and Libyans a mighty army with
great numbers of chariots and horsemen? Yet when you
relied on the Lord, he delivered them into your hand. For the
eyes of the Lord range throughout the earth to strengthen
those whose hearts are fully committed to him."*
2 Chronicles 16:8–9 niv

Do the tasks before you seem too much for your flagging energy?
Are you wondering how to teach your children, help the hurting,
or feed the hungry, when you're just not enough?

A little boy long ago may have also believed that his small
offering to Jesus probably wouldn't make a big difference. After
all there were over five thousand people and all he had was one
small lunch—two fish and five loaves. But instead of holding
back what seemed insignificant in the face of such great need,
he gave what he had to Jesus.

Jesus promised that His load is light and His burden easy.
Whatever you're facing that seems too much for your strength,
give Him your hands for the work. Bring Him your fish and bread,
and trust Him for the increase.

*Lord, give me the strength to remain faithful.
I offer to You what little I have. Amen.*

GOD USES YOUR FAITH TO MAKE THINGS HAPPEN

Jesus said to them, Do you believe that I am able to do this? They said to Him, Yes, Lord. Then He touched their eyes, saying, According to your faith and trust and reliance [on the power invested in Me] be it done to you; and their eyes were opened.
MATTHEW 9:28–30 AMPC

Jesus asked two blind men, "Do you think I'm able to do this?" They answered yes, prompting Him to touch their eyes, saying, "Because of your faith, it will happen" (Matthew 9:29 NLT). And they regained their sight!

Later, Jesus was in His hometown of Nazareth, teaching in the synagogue there. But "because of their unbelief, he couldn't do any miracles among them except to place his hands on a few sick people and heal them" (Mark 6:5 NLT; see also Matthew 13:58). The wonders Jesus works belong only to people who believe or are ready to believe in Him and His power.

God loves you and wants to work miracles in your life. And He will do so according to your faith!

*I believe in You, Lord! I trust in Your power.
Work a wonder in my life. In Jesus' name, amen!*

CONFIDENT HOPE

*What is faith? It is the confident assurance that something we
want is going to happen. It is the certainty that what we hope
for is waiting for us, even though we cannot see it up ahead.*
HEBREWS 11:1 TLB

What do you believe about God? Do you believe that He tells
the truth? Do you believe He is reliable? Good? Just? It's vitally
important to spend some time evaluating just exactly what you
believe about His character because your beliefs form the lens
through which you see life. The deeper your understanding of
His goodness and strength and wisdom, the better you will rightly
interpret His ultimate purpose for your life.

If you believe that life is short, that eternity is long, and that
God is good even though life is hard, you'll learn the value of
perseverance and the power of God's promises.

*God, I believe in Your goodness and truth. I believe that
everything You have promised us will happen just like You said.
I believe that a fantastic eternity with You awaits! Amen.*

GOD TURNS YOUR NEGATIVES INTO POSITIVES

*We are destroying speculations and every lofty thing
raised up against the knowledge of God, and we are
taking every thought captive to the obedience of Christ.*
2 Corinthians 10:5 nasb

When you think you cannot do the impossible, Jesus tells you,
"If you had faith even as small as a mustard seed, you could say
to this mountain, 'Move from here to there,' and it would move.
Nothing would be impossible" (Matthew 17:20 nlt). When you
think no one loves you, God says He does (see Zephaniah 3:17).
When you think you don't have the strength, God says you can do
all things through Christ who gives you strength (see Philippians 4:13). When you think you'll never get rid of your burden or
that no one cares about you, Jesus tells you to cast your burden
on Him; He'll carry it because *He* cares for you (see 1 Peter 5:7).

*Lord, please make me more aware of what I'm thinking.
And if any negative thoughts come up, prompt me to take them
to Christ and replace them with Your truth! Transform me, Lord!*

Day 294

STEP OUT

*Don't become so well-adjusted to your culture that you fit into it
without even thinking. Instead, fix your attention on God. You'll
be changed from the inside out. Readily recognize what he wants
from you, and quickly respond to it. Unlike the culture around
you, always dragging you down to its level of immaturity, God
brings the best out of you, develops well-formed maturity in you.*
ROMANS 12:2 MSG

Peter walked on water when he accepted Jesus' invitation to
"Come." What if Jesus asked you not to merely rock the world's
comfortable boat, but to step out of it. Would you respond to
His leading? Sure, Peter sank a little when he took his eyes off
Jesus for a moment, but then he cried out to Jesus immediately.
And Jesus immediately reached out to him. If you waver in the
radical life of a disciple, call out, "Jesus, I need Your help right
now!" He's got you. Just like He always has. And through His
supernatural power you *can* live His best for you.

*Lord, give me courage and faith to step out onto the
water with You, to radically follow Your leading. Amen.*

GOD WILL CONTINUALLY GUIDE AND RESTORE YOU

"Feed the hungry, and help those in trouble. Then your light will shine out from the darkness, and the darkness around you will be as bright as noon. The LORD will guide you continually, giving you water when you are dry and restoring your strength."
ISAIAH 58:10–11 NLT

God doesn't want you to live merely to satisfy your desires. If you have truly accepted Christ, you'll want to do for others.

When you serve others as Jesus served you, God promises you'll shine bright. And God will give you continual guidance, quench your thirst and hunger, and restore your strength. As you bless, God will bless you and your efforts over and over again! You are a precious one who is walking in His light, taking care of those precious to Him who can no longer take care of themselves. It's a three-way win!

I want to serve You by serving others, Lord. Show me what You would have me do and who You want me to serve. I know You'll give me all the resources and strength to do whatever task You put upon my heart.

A HELPER

*"But the Helper, the Holy Spirit, whom the Father will
send in my name, he will teach you all things and bring
to your remembrance all that I have said to you."*
JOHN 14:26 ESV

How many times have you wished to clone yourself because life
is so overwhelming? Even though we don't have clones running
around to help us, we're never alone.

When it was time for Jesus to return to heaven to be with the
Father, He made sure the disciples knew they still had a friend
around to help them. That helper is the Holy Spirit. And as believers, His Spirit dwells in us.

When you're wishing there were two of you to tackle your
troubles, remember you've got a friend. The Holy Spirit knows
the answers to all your questions about living God's plans for you.

*Holy Spirit, I need help today. Fill me with Your supernatural
power to resist temptations and please God with my actions. Amen.*

GOD WANTS YOU TO SEEK HIM EARLY

*I love those who love me, and those who seek me early and
diligently shall find me. . . . For whoever finds me [Wisdom]
finds life and draws forth and obtains favor from the Lord.*
PROVERBS 8:17, 35 AMPC

God wants to be in on everything you're thinking about and
planning. He wants you to come to Him so He can help, guide,
inspire, and provide you with all the resources you'll need. And
the best time of day for you to come to Him is in the early morning hours, before the rest of the house awakes.

Begin your day with God. Seek His face. Peruse His Word.
And most important of all, pray—for every need you have, every
task before you, every person you'll encounter, every desire
you'd like Him to bless. As you seek God, you'll find Him. Have
no doubt about that!

> *Lord, thank You for spending time with me.
> Here's how my day looks. . . . Please bless my
> efforts and give me all I need as I live in You.*

LIVE WHAT YOU BELIEVE

*All Scripture is breathed out by God and profitable for teaching,
for reproof, for correction, and for training in righteousness, that
the man of God may be complete, equipped for every good work.*
2 TIMOTHY 3:16–17 ESV

I go to church and read my Bible. I say that Jesus is my Lord,
but what really happens when life hits me head-on? When my
kids exhaust me? When the line at the grocery store is too long,
or when I lose my keys when I'm already late? Do I calmly send
up a prayer? Or do I lash out in anger?

As we reflect on our behavior, we should be so grateful for
God's mercy. Our lives are also proof of what we really believe.
And our lives should offer solid evidence that we follow after
Jesus. Can I get an amen?

*Lord, use my time in Your Word to prepare me for the day
ahead. Do life with me today. Help me to resist sin—to do
Your will and not mine in each moment of this day. Amen.*

GOD'S ANGEL SURROUNDS, GUARDS, AND RESCUES YOU

This poor man cried, and the Lord heard him, and saved
him out of all his troubles. The Angel of the Lord encamps
around those who fear Him [who revere and worship
Him with awe] and each of them He delivers.
PSALM 34:6–7 AMPC

When you are in trouble, when you are desperate, when you see no way out, cry to God. Pray for His help. And Yahweh Himself the most powerful of all beings—will rescue you, deliver you from all that's coming against you.

God will set up a circle of protection around you so that nothing will reach you or harm you. Why? Because you, whom He loves, cried out to Him. Like a loving father who will do anything to protect His little one, God the Father is ready to put everything on the line to get you out of whatever straits you are in. Just call, and Yahweh will be there.

I stand amazed, Lord, at the lengths You,
the all-powerful one, will go to when I find myself in a
desperate situation, at the power You'll so willingly expend
on my behalf. Thank You, Lord, for loving me so much!

THE RIGHT PURSUITS

Flee youthful passions and pursue righteousness, faith, love, and peace, along with those who call on the Lord from a pure heart. Have nothing to do with foolish, ignorant controversies; you know that they breed quarrels. And the Lord's servant must not be quarrelsome but kind to everyone, able to teach, patiently enduring evil, correcting his opponents with gentleness.

2 TIMOTHY 2:22–25 ESV

What have you been pursuing recently? We pursue many things for even more reasons. We chase down fitness one mile at a time. We sprint after entertainment and pleasurable activities. Some of us run after fame, wealth, enlightenment, or knowledge.

But what about righteousness? Have you planned to please God today? Have you set right living, faith, love, and peace before you and run toward those goals intentionally? If you haven't, there's great news. Today is a fresh start! Don't pursue empty endeavors that lead to spiritual death. You won't be filled by running after other things. God is the only one who can fill you up with life and joy.

*Lord, help me turn away from sin today
and pursue righteousness. Amen.*

GOD, YOUR ABBA, HAS ADOPTED YOU

God sent him to buy freedom for us who were slaves to the law, so that he could adopt us as his very own children. And because we are his children, God has sent the Spirit of his Son into our hearts, prompting us to call out, "Abba, Father." Now you are. . .God's own child. . . . [H]is heir.
GALATIANS 4:5–7 NLT

When Jesus died for you, allowing you to be forgiven your mistakes, you automatically became a part of God's forever family. Because the almighty Lord has adopted you as His very own little girl, He has sent the Spirit of Jesus into your heart. You are now the heir to His promises and have access to all His blessings. When you realize all these blessings and benefits, you can't help but call out, "Abba, Father!"

Abba is the Aramaic term that can be translated as Daddy. Feel Abba's Spirit deep within you. Snuggle up to His warmth and compassion. Delight in His presence as He reaches out to embrace you in His arms of love.

Abba! Daddy God! Thank You for adopting me.
My heart is full of joy. I want to jump into Your
arms. Hold me, Abba. Keep me close.

Day 302

GOD IS GOOD

*Open your mouth and taste, open your eyes and see—
how good God is. Blessed are you who run to him.*
PSALM 34:8 MSG

God is pure, unadulterated goodness. Yes, tragic and terrible things have happened on this earth, but God is still patiently working out His plan so that each one of us might be saved. Hardships may come in this world, but all His promises will be kept—though some not until we reach heaven.

Take His nail-scarred hand, and trust in His ability to work out the rough places in your eternal favor. Trust in His far-reaching gaze that sees both the beginning and the end. If His intentions for us were shaded by anything less than utter goodness, He would not have sent His precious Son into our war-torn world to save us.

*God, You are the only one who is truly good. I trust
You with my present and my future. Amen.*

Day 303

GOD'S WORD GIVES YOU SUPERNATURAL INSIGHT

You, through Your commandments, make me wiser than
my enemies, for [Your words] are ever before me.
Psalm 119:98 ampc

When Solomon became king, God appeared to him in a dream and asked, "What do you want? Ask, and I will give it to you!" (1 Kings 3:5 nlt). Solomon explained that even though he was king, he was still a child who didn't know his way around. So he asked God to give him an understanding heart so he could rule His people well. God was so pleased that He gave Solomon not only wisdom but riches and fame!

Your greatest source for wisdom is found in God's Word. As you read, study, and meditate upon it, you'll gain more understanding and deeper insight than your teachers and elders. It will also keep you on God's good path.

I want and need the wisdom and supernatural insight that only
You can provide, Lord. Show me where You would have me
start my search within Your Word. Lead me by Your Spirit.

LOVE NEVER ENDS

*If I speak in the tongues of men and of angels, but have not love,
I am a noisy gong or a clanging cymbal. And if I have prophetic
powers, and understand all mysteries and all knowledge, and if I have
all faith, so as to remove mountains, but have not love, I am nothing.
If I give away all I have, and if I deliver up my body to be burned, but
have not love, I gain nothing. Love is patient and kind; love does not
envy or boast; it is not arrogant or rude. It does not insist on its own
way; it is not irritable or resentful; it does not rejoice at wrongdoing,
but rejoices with the truth. Love bears all things, believes all
things, hopes all things, endures all things. Love never ends.*
1 CORINTHIANS 13:1–8 ESV

We've all patted misty eyes at weddings when the words of 1 Corinthians 13 have perfumed the atmosphere with the paramount power of love. And it *is* the perfect foundation for a solid marriage. But Paul wrote these words not to a blushing bride in white but to the bride of Christ—the church.

Sometimes we strive to make big gestures for Jesus and neglect the everyday moments. But Paul says you can give your life and all your possessions yet not gain a thing if you fail to love the people around you. Love well today.

*Lord, teach me Your love. Show me how to
release it during every moment I live. Amen.*

GOD WILL NEVER DISAPPOINT YOU

The LORD answered me and said, "Record the vision and inscribe it on tablets, that the one who reads it may run. For the vision is yet for the appointed time; it hastens toward the goal and it will not fail. Though it tarries, wait for it; for it will certainly come, it will not delay."

HABAKKUK 2:2–3 NASB

When you pour out your heart to God and ask Him for a vision, an answer, a plan, He wants you to be patient as you await the answer He'll provide by His Word, Spirit, or providence. He won't disappoint you or your expectations when you patiently wait to hear from Him or see evidence of His answer. Though your blessing may take a long while in reaching you, it will finally come, and its timing will be perfect.

Be patient in God. He won't disappoint you.

I'm keeping the faith, Lord, patiently waiting for and expecting a word, a sign, an answer from You. I know Your timing will be perfect.

Day 306

HOME

Our citizenship is in heaven, and from it
we await a Savior, the Lord Jesus Christ.
PHILIPPIANS 3:20 ESV

Our house isn't truly home for us. On this earth we're promised trouble. Wars, smooth-talking politicians, a national obsession with overeating on one extreme and the perfect body on the other, the daily grind of living upright in a sin-steeped culture—these things should leave us longing for a different place.

If your only hope lies in this world, you're going to be disappointed. Your soul will remain unsatisfied as you look around for what's missing. But that elusive piece is not of this world. You can find it only in Jesus and His kingdom—a place where Jesus waits to embrace you in love. The place your soul calls home.

Lord, this earth, fallen as it is, is familiar to me.
Help me resist the temptation to cling to this place.
I do long to be at home with You. Amen.

GOD GIVES YOU RESISTANCE

*So be subject to God. Resist the devil [stand
firm against him], and he will flee from you.
Come close to God and He will come close to you.*

JAMES 4:7–8 AMPC

The Bible makes it clear that you cannot serve two masters, both
God and mammon (see Matthew 6:24). You cannot be a friend
of the world and of God at the same time (see James 4:4).

When you choose submitting to God instead of the world,
you can stand firm against the evil one. He'll flee from you. As
God works His will in you, you'll be able to shout no to the devil,
and he'll take off. A mere whisper of yes to God will bring Him
running to your side. The best route, the eternal road is with
God. For as you "humble yourselves before the Lord. . .he will
lift you up in honor" (James 4:10 NLT).

*Lord, I don't want to be double-minded.
Help me to stay humble, to follow Your
plan and path. I want to please You alone.*

GOD OFFERS HEALING

*When Jesus noticed him lying there [helpless],
knowing that he had already been a long time in
that condition, He said to him, Do you want to become
well? [Are you really in earnest about getting well?]*
JOHN 5:6 AMPC

Jesus went to the Bethesda pool where the first people to get into the water were healed from their affliction. By that pool was a man who'd been sick for thirty-eight years. Jesus asked him, "Do you want to get well?" The man said he couldn't get well because he had no one to help him get into the water in time. Jesus told him to stand up, pick up his mat, and walk. At His words, the man was healed!

God offers you total healing of all your ills. Trust this: He *will* make you whole. He'd never do anything less.

*I know I have some problems and worries that I've not
been letting You handle, Lord. No more excuses. I turn
myself completely over to You. Make me whole.*

BECOMING RIGHTEOUS

*For our sake he made him to be sin who knew no sin,
so that in him we might become the righteousness of God.*
2 CORINTHIANS 5:21 ESV

Jesus stepped down from His place in glory for a time to live a perfect life and die a perfect sacrifice for our sins to restore us—sinful, fallen humans—to the relationship God created us for.

Because of Jesus' blood, God doesn't see a sin-stained human when He looks at you. Jesus died to pay our price. To blot out our sins. To satisfy heaven's wrath. So that we could be adorned in His righteousness before God. No, loved one, He doesn't see your mess ups, wrong motives, or prideful moments; He sees His daughter. And you are dressed in the pure-white borrowed righteousness of Jesus.

*Father, thank You for making me Your beloved child.
Not just a sinner You've let in as the black sheep of
the family, but Your precious daughter. Amen.*

GOD WANTS YOU TO BE HIS HANDS AND FEET

*Now you [collectively] are Christ's body and [individually]
you are members of it, each part severally and distinct
[each with his own place and function].*
1 CORINTHIANS 12:27 AMPC

You're a unique woman, God's masterpiece. You've been created anew in Jesus. And God has given you a special assignment, a purpose only you can live out.

Do not doubt that you can do what you've been called to do. For God has prepared you for every good work (see 2 Timothy 3:17). It's all been prearranged by Him. Everything is in place. Pray that God would reveal His mission for you, show you the steps to take, reveal the work ahead. Then walk in His will and way with all the confidence a daughter of the King should have.

*Lord, I'm ready. Reveal the gift You want me to use to serve
You, to be Your heavenly hands and feet on this earth.*

LIVING IT UP

*My God will supply every need of yours according
to his riches in glory in Christ Jesus. To our God and
Father be glory forever and ever. Amen.*
PHILIPPIANS 4:19–20 ESV

Does this verse in Philippians mean that we will never go hungry
and obtain every desire that flits through our minds?

Paul was sending encouragement and thanks to the Phi-
lippian church for their sacrificial giving to support him. He
encouraged them that because they had put their faith in
action, he was certain that God will take care of them. They gave
generously. . .over and over.

Maybe God has not blessed you with worldly wealth, but He
will surely supply "every need." And what He has given already
is so much more than mere financial assistance. Through His
Son, He has supplied the needs of your eternal soul.

*Lord, Your Word says that when I give, it will be given
to me. I know that when I trust You and give generously
to help others, You supply all my needs. Amen.*

Day 312

GOD WILL STRAIGHTEN
YOU OUT

*There was a woman there who for eighteen years had
had an infirmity caused by a spirit (a demon of sickness).
She was bent completely forward and utterly unable
to straighten herself up or to look upward.*
LUKE 13:11 AMPC

Jesus said to the woman, "You are released from your infirmity!"
(Luke 13:12 AMPC). He then laid His hands on her, and she was
instantly straight! Right away "she recognized. . .and praised
God" (Luke 13:13 AMPC).

There will be times when you cannot lift yourself up or
straighten yourself out no matter how hard you try. That's
when you need to seek out Jesus to release you from whatever
has bent you over. One word from Him and you're made right
again, able to once more look up and praise God. Seek out Jesus. And the combination of your faith and God's restorative
power will heal whatever ails you, straighten out whatever you
cannot, prompting you to look up and praise the Master Healer.

*There is something I cannot do in my own power, Lord. So I bring
my faith and my malady to You, ready for Your healing touch.*

BECAUSE OF YOUR LOVE

Always be humble and gentle. Be patient with each other,
making allowance for each other's faults because of your love.
EPHESIANS 4:2 NLT

If your life was known by one thing, what would it be? Humility? Patience? Love? It seems that too often we are known by our divisions instead of our love, even within the walls of the church. We complain, we accuse, we hold grudges. Instead of making allowances for one another's shortcomings, we judge. Instead of encouraging, we tear down.

But the identifying marker of our Christianity is supposed to be our love. Because of your love, be humble and gentle. Because of your love, be patient. Because of your love, make allowances and bear with one another. After all, we love because of His love. Today, may everyone know whose you are—because of your love.

Father, may Your love pour from me today.
When I'm tempted to respond in a less than
loving way, help me hold back my words. Amen.

GOD REWARDS YOUR SINCERE SEEKING OF HIM

Without faith it is impossible to please and be satisfactory to Him. For whoever would come near to God must [necessarily] believe that God exists and that He is the rewarder of those who earnestly and diligently seek Him [out].

HEBREWS 11:6 AMPC

Noah followed God's directions and built an ark. Because of his faithfulness, God saved him and his family while the rest of the world was wiped out by a catastrophic flood. Abraham and Sarah, because of their faith, were rewarded with a son in their old age. Motivated by faith, Moses led the Israelites out of Egypt, never wavering in His purpose.

You too have all the qualities and resources you need to be a woman of faith. Seek God, believe and trust in Him, and follow Him, even when you're not sure where He's taking you. As you do, you will be rewarded.

Lord, I firmly believe You exist and reward those who earnestly seek You. May my faith be pleasing in Your sight!

FUTURE GLORY

*Yet what we suffer now is nothing compared to the glory he
will reveal to us later. For all creation is waiting eagerly for that
future day when God will reveal who his children really are.*
ROMANS 8:18–19 NLT

Don't lose sight of the goal. Remember what you're waiting
for. All God's amazing promises to us are "Yes!" But we live in
the *not yet*. "All the promises of God find their Yes in him" (2
Corinthians 1:20 ESV). Our timeline doesn't always line up with
His. Our perception of time is skewed because we're human
and He's God.

But if all creation is eagerly waiting for this day, why are we
not also on the edge of our seats? Today, focus on what you're
waiting for. You're mere steps from the wonder of eternity.

Lord, keep my eyes focused on future glory. Amen.

Day 316

GOD'S SPIRIT REDIRECTS YOU

Next Paul and Silas traveled through the area of Phrygia and Galatia, because the Holy Spirit had prevented them from preaching the word in the province of Asia at that time.
ACTS 16:6 NLT

Paul and Silas had a plan, but the Holy Spirit redirected them from Asia, so they went to another area. When they came to the borders of Mysia, they headed north, "but again the Spirit of Jesus did not allow them to go there" (Acts 16:7 NLT). That night, Paul had a vision of a man begging him to go to Macedonia, so they decided to head there right away.

Although you have plans, there will be times when God's Spirit redirects you. For your sake and God's glory, be open to His promptings. He'll never steer you wrong.

*I'm determined to be open in heart, mind, body,
and soul to Your Spirit's direction. My goal is
to allow Your plans to override my own.*

DO YOU TRUST HIM?

*You will keep in perfect peace those whose minds
are steadfast, because they trust in you.*
ISAIAH 26:3 NIV

The meaning of the Hebrew word for *steadfast* in this verse is "to support or brace, to uphold." If our minds are upheld and supported by the truth of who God really is and our trust in Him, we will experience perfect peace.

Do you trust God? Do you trust Him to know more about your future than you do? Do you trust Him when you're hurting? Do you trust Him when times get tough? Can you trust His absolute goodness and good plans enough to give Him carte blanche over your life? What about the lives of the people you care about?

Beloved, all you have to do today is trust.

*Lord, You are God. I trust in Your good plans.
Thank You for enfolding me in peace. Amen.*

GOD'S WORD GROUNDS
AND BLESSES YOU

He said to Simon (Peter), Put out into the deep [water], and lower
your nets for a haul. And Simon (Peter) answered, Master,
we toiled all night [exhaustingly] and caught nothing [in our nets].
But on the ground of Your word, I will lower the nets [again].
LUKE 5:4–5 AMPC

Jesus told Peter to take the boat into the deeper waters and lower
his nets. Peter explained how they'd fished all night long and
hadn't caught a thing. But He did what Jesus said.

And then. . .he and his fellow fishermen caught so many
fish that their nets were beginning to tear. They asked other
fishermen in another boat to help them and filled both the
boats with so many fish they were at the point of sinking. When
they reached shore, the fishermen left all to join Jesus.

When you ground yourself on Jesus' Word, following His
commands and promptings, even though they go against logic,
you too will find an abundance of blessings.

I want You to be Lord of my life, Jesus. May I follow
Your promptings even if I don't really understand them.
For whenever I do, I know I will find a boatload of blessings.

Day 319
SALTY SPEECH

*Walk in wisdom toward outsiders, making the best use of the
time. Let your speech always be gracious, seasoned with salt,
so that you may know how you ought to answer each person.*
COLOSSIANS 4:5–6 ESV

Our time here is limited, and the world is watching. Scripture
tells us to use wisdom when interacting with unbelievers, treating
every moment as precious. Have you ever considered that the
words you choose and the example you live could influence the
eternal destination of the people around you?

Grace is magnetic. Season your words and deeds generously
with it, and others will be attracted to the banquet you've spread
before them. Don't cut down, criticize, or judge other people—
that's not the job Jesus gave you. He charged you to be salt, a tasty
preservative in a dying world.

Be kind and gentle in all you say today, so others will be
drawn to God's transformative grace.

*Father, give me wisdom, love, and self-control as I interact with
the world. Let the words that I say and the things that
I do lead them to a life of belonging to You
our good and perfect Father. Amen.*

GOD SEES YOUR NEED
AND MOVES TO MEET IT

A funeral procession was coming out as he approached
the village gate. The young man who had died was a
widow's only son, and a large crowd from the village
was with her. When the Lord saw her, his heart
overflowed with compassion. "Don't cry!" he said.
LUKE 7:12–13 NLT

Jesus and His disciples were walking to the village of Nain. It was there He saw a funeral procession. A young man, the bereaved widow's only son and support, had died. When Jesus saw her, His heart gushed with compassion for her. His only words to her were, "Don't cry!" He then went over to the coffin and placed His hands upon it. Jesus told the young man to get up (see Luke 7:14 NLT). The boy sat up and began talking!

Jesus sees what you're up against. His heart goes out to you and overflows with compassion and empathy. He knows what You need even when you don't ask Him for anything. Have faith. Expect Him to move.

You move me, Lord. Thank You for seeing,
caring for, and moving in my life.

TRANSFORMED BY TRIALS

We are hard pressed on every side, but not crushed;
perplexed, but not in despair; persecuted, but not
abandoned; struck down, but not destroyed.
2 CORINTHIANS 4:8 9 NIV

Friend, have you been wounded deeply? Has bitterness set its roots in your soul? Jesus understands wounds. He was laughed at, spat upon, betrayed, and denied. And then He was beaten and pierced. But being broken wasn't the end of His story. And our brokenness is not the end of ours either.

No one wants to experience faith-testing hardships, but God can redeem every moment of our pain to transform us. As we are broken open and exposed to the living water, the bitterness leaches out of our human hearts, and we are made useful for His good purpose.

Father, uphold me on the hard days.
I know that in my brokenness and difficulties,
You're forming a heart ready for service. Amen.

GOD PROVIDES YOU A SECRET PLACE

He who dwells in the secret place of the Most High shall
remain stable and fixed under the shadow of the Almighty
[Whose power no foe can withstand]. I will say of the
Lord, He is my Refuge and my Fortress, my God; on Him
I lean and rely, and in Him I [confidently] trust!
PSALM 91:1–2 AMPC

What is this "secret place"? It's a place where you reside with
the God who is all mighty, "Whose power no foe can with-
stand"—seen or unseen. Where you're safe under His "shadow," a
metaphor for His care and protection. Where you affirm aloud,
"The Lord is my Refuge"—a place of security. "The Lord is my
Fortress"—protection from attack. "In Him I lean and rely on
and totally trust Him."

Dwell in the secret place of God, and find the respite your
soul longs for. As you do, He will deliver you, love you, and honor
you. You have nothing to lose and everything to gain!

Lord, today I come to You, ready to live in that
secret place of peace, protection, and love.

Day 323

FINDING PEACE

Do not be anxious about anything, but in everything by prayer and
supplication with thanksgiving let your requests be made known
to God. And the peace of God, which surpasses all understanding,
will guard your hearts and your minds in Christ Jesus.

PHILIPPIANS 4:6–7 ESV

The antidote for Satan's cycle of psychological warfare is thanks-giving. Philippians says that giving thanks results in peace. Unimaginable peace. Restful peace.

The process goes like this. First you need something to be thankful about. So pause and look around. Find one thing to thank God for. Then thank Him for it. And then find another and thank Him for that too. While you are thanking your Father in heaven, you will begin to see Him moving around you. And suddenly you will realize you are not alone. A dawning realization will break upon your mind—God is truly in control. He really does have this! And the peace that surpasses all understanding will wash over you.

God, thank You for another day to love You.
Thank You for peace in this place. Amen.

Day 324

GOD GIVES YOU
SECOND CHANCES

*"I sank beneath the waves, and the waters closed over
me. Seaweed wrapped itself around my head. . . . As my
life was slipping away, I remembered the Lord. And my
earnest prayer went out to you in your holy Temple."*
JONAH 2:5, 7 NLT

God told Jonah to go to Nineveh and announce His judgment
upon the wicked city. But Jonah ran away. He boarded a ship that
was headed in the opposite direction. God created a huge storm
that was only calmed by the sailors throwing Jonah into the sea,
and then God caused a huge fish to swallow Jonah.

While down in the fish's belly, Jonah prayed for deliverance,
so God had the fish vomit him onto the shore. Then Jonah decided it was best to obey God. He went to Nineveh and shared
God's message.

When you disobey God, there's no doubt you'll feel consequences of your original waywardness. Yet, because of His great
compassion, God will give you a second chance. Your mission:
Take it!

*Show me, Lord, where I might have missed
an opportunity to serve You. Then, in Your
compassion, please give me a second chance!*

TURN AWAY FROM SIN

Point out anything in me that offends you,
and lead me along the path of everlasting life.
PSALM 139:24 NLT

Clara slammed the pot onto the stovetop. She couldn't believe her friend said that to her. She dropped some silverware into the dishwasher and shoved the rack back inside. Her kids glanced at her from the living room, and her husband's eyebrow arced into his hairline. She knew she was letting her emotions run wild, but those words stung.

Sin is like a fast-spreading cancer to our hearts. God doesn't want you to cover it up and pretend it won't kill you. He wants you to acknowledge it, confess it, and turn away from it. When your attitude starts to stink, ask God to reveal to you the source of your offending behavior.

Lord, show me when my actions disappoint You.
Forgive me for sinning against You, and teach me
to live in a way that's pleasing to You. Amen.

GOD LIFTS YOU HIGHER

*Hear my cry, O God; give heed to my prayer. From the
end of the earth I call to You when my heart is faint;
lead me to the rock that is higher than I. For You have been
a refuge for me, a tower of strength against the enemy.*
PSALM 61:1–3 NASB

When you're in dire straits, when you are overwhelmed, when you're weak of body and faint of heart and spirit, when you can't seem to get out of your own head, you need God. He's the only one who can give you a new perspective, shield you from the darkness, cover you with His peace, deliver you from your enemies, and give you the breathing room you need.

As God lifted Moses and put him in a cleft of the rock as His glory passed by (see Exodus 33:22), God will lift you and settle you down on that rock, that "higher place" you cannot reach, keeping you safe until you're once again secure in Him, your strength regained, your heart at peace, and your vision clear.

*Lord, I need Your strength, peace,
and safety. Lift me to that high rock.*

Day 327
FIND SPACE FOR HIM

Many are the plans in the mind of a man,
but it is the purpose of the Lord that will stand.
PROVERBS 19:21 ESV

Sometimes the day morphs into something that just happens to us, like getting steamrolled. Instead of a faithful life lived on purpose, we're dragged around by our overcrammed schedules. In the end there's not much left for the good things in life, and we come out feeling a bit mauled—and we forget to find the good path God would lead us down under all that activity.

Do you need to plan for a bit more margin in your day? Because if you don't leave free space in your life, how can you expect to be available for God's business of the day? After all, when we see Jesus, I don't think He'll be impressed with the size of our day planners.

Heavenly Father, forgive me for scheduling
You right out of my day. My time belongs
to You. Help me to use it wisely. Amen.

GOD SPEAKS IN YOUR SILENCE

*For God alone my soul waits in silence; from Him comes my
salvation. He only is my Rock and my Salvation, my Defense
and my Fortress. . . . My soul, wait only upon God and silently
submit to Him; for my hope and expectation are from Him.*
PSALM 62:1–2, 5 AMPC

The world is a very noisy place, full of distractions. When you
attempt to sit down with God, the noise of traffic, people's voices,
TVs blaring, and barking dogs can seep through. Once you get
yourself to ignore those sounds, the internal dialogue begins
as you start thinking about all the phone calls, emails, and texts
you need to respond to and the to-do list you're determined to
complete. With all that's going on, it's hard to find a moment of
peace, much less silence. But silence—within and without—is what
you need to hear God speak (see Zephaniah 1:7; Habakkuk 2:20).
For God isn't in all the noise. He's "[a sound of gentle stillness
and] a still, small voice" (1 Kings 19:12 AMPC).

*My soul, wait in silence before God, for He
alone brings hope, peace, and a good word.*

Day 329
WASH ME—AGAIN

*Then one of the elders addressed me, saying, "Who are these,
clothed in white robes, and from where have they come?"
I said to him, "Sir, you know." And he said to me, "These are
the ones coming out of the great tribulation. They have washed
their robes and made them white in the blood of the Lamb."*
REVELATION 7:13–14 ESV

Let's think about washing for a moment. I used to be a dirty rag
in need of a firm scrub. And even though I now belong to God
and my grime has been washed away by His blood and I've been
declared righteous in His eyes, in this life I still stain myself
with selfishness, pride, impatience, and unkind words. I mess
up and cause hurt. I have faults. I still need the churning of the
Holy Spirit to wake up my conscience and point out where I've
got mud on my heart.

Lord, keep washing me and making me more like Jesus. Amen.

GOD GIVES YOU SANCTUARY

*But when I considered how to understand this, it was
too great an effort for me and too painful until I went
into the sanctuary of God; then I understood.*
PSALM 73:16–17 AMPC

Sometimes there are some life questions that you just can't
figure out. You try to let them go, but they just keep coming
back into your mind. When this happens, the first and best
path for you is to go to God's sanctuary. For you, this may be
your church or your prayer closet (see Matthew 6:6) where you
meet alone with God.

You really don't even have to pose your question. God already knows what's on your mind. And while you're in His
presence, focusing on Him, you can be sure God will guide you
with His counsel (see Psalm 73:24). And while you're there, He'll
strengthen your heart as well (see Psalm 73:26).

*Lord, I have a question that's been on my mind lately.
And I can't seem to find the answer, so here I am before You.
Help me understand, and then strengthen my heart.*

FAITH ACTS

Does merely talking about faith indicate that a person really has it? For instance, you come upon an old friend dressed in rags and half-starved and say, "Good morning, friend! Be clothed in Christ! Be filled with the Holy Spirit!" and walk off without providing so much as a coat or a cup of soup—where does that get you? Isn't it obvious that God-talk without God-acts is outrageous nonsense? . . . Do you suppose for a minute that you can cut faith and works in two and not end up with a corpse on your hands?

James 2:14–17, 20 msg

As a believer in Jesus, you're living the most hope-filled, loved life you could ever imagine. God—as in the God *of this universe—* loves you. Yes, He loves flawed, sometimes unfaithful, falling-apart you—with a deep, passionate, and limitless love. He walked out of heaven and died a horrible death just to fling open the doors of eternal paradise for you. Because you're His.

But what He doesn't want is for you to selfishly hoard this perspective-shattering, world-altering knowledge and go about your business as if it were yesterday's back-page advertisement.

Is your faith alive and thriving in loving action today?

Father, thank You for loving me so completely.
Because I am loved I can love others. Amen.

GOD NOURISHES YOU WITH HIDDEN MANNA

I have food (nourishment) to eat of which you know nothing and have no idea. . . . My food (nourishment) is to do the will (pleasure) of Him Who sent Me and to accomplish and completely finish His work.
JOHN 4:32, 34 AMPC

Jesus and the disciples had been walking a long way. The disciples went to buy food. And even though Jesus was totally exhausted, He had a long conversation with a Samaritan woman and changed her life!

When the disciples urged Jesus to eat the food they'd brought, He said He had food they knew nothing about! They wondered if someone else had brought Him food while they'd been gone. But Jesus explained that His nourishment came from doing God's will!

You also have access to God's hidden manna. Thus, even when you're weary, don't shrink from doing God's work, the things that please Him. For as soon as you begin, God will not only nourish but revive and refresh your mind, body, spirit, and soul!

*I want to please You, Lord. So even when
I'm tired, I will seek to do Your will, knowing You
will supply all the nourishment I need as I do so.*

FRUIT OF HIS LABOR

*Blessed is everyone who fears the Lord, who walks in his
ways! You shall eat the fruit of the labor of your hands;
you shall be blessed, and it shall be well with you.*
Psalm 128:1–2 esv

Annabelle swiped a trickle of sweat from her forehead and sat
back on her heels, tired but satisfied. Her small garden plot was
brimming with produce. She had spent many hours here on her
knees—weeding, pruning, watering, and, most important, talking
with her Creator. She had cultivated her precious relationship
with the one she belonged to with the same daily dedication
that she had poured out to her little garden patch. And now her
vegetables were mature and delicious to all who were hungry.
Annabelle prayed that her life would be as nourishing to those
hungry souls in the world as her homegrown vegetables.

Have you allowed the Holy Spirit to till the ground of your
heart and pull out the weeds?

*Lord, teach me Your ways. Bless me with growth and
abundant fruit so I can spread hope in this world. Amen.*

GOD SHOWS YOU THE PATH OF LIFE

I said to the LORD, "You are my Master! Every good
thing I have comes from you." . . . You will show me
the way of life, granting me the joy of your presence
and the pleasures of living with you forever.
PSALM 16:2, 11 NLT

God is delighted to show you the way of life in Him. He counsels you in His Word, prompts you through the Holy Spirit, and has given you Jesus as an example so you'll know the way He wants you to go. Thus, when you come to a fork in the road, God, your eternal guide, will give you all the direction you need to keep you on the right road, leading you to the ramp that leads to His presence and delight while you're on the earth and the one you'll proceed upon after death as you ride on into heaven. "For this God is our God forever and ever; He will be our guide [even] until death" (Psalm 48:14 AMPC).

Help me, Lord, to be alert to Your signals and
signposts as I ride this eternal way of life with You!

Day 335

REMADE

He gives snow like wool; he scatters frost like ashes.
PSALM 147:16 ESV

Before we have Jesus in our world, we're broken and dead, brown and dirty. We can't hope to be any better than we are, so we're left with no hope at all. But then Jesus takes our messy lives and gives us His righteousness to wear. He drapes a robe of white right over that dirty mess of impatience, anger, bitterness, and an endless line of mistakes.

He spoke our world into existence, and now He studies the empty canvas of a new life in Him. He lifts His brush, and with gentle strokes He paints a new picture of love, faithfulness, hope, and forgiveness. The Creator of the world creates a heart like His in you.

Jesus, thank You for covering my shame in the purity of white—in the undeserved glory of Your righteousness. I belong to You. Make my heart look like Yours. Amen.

Day 336

GOD WILL NEVER LET YOU BE SHAKEN

I have set the Lord continually before me; because He is at my right hand, I will not be shaken. Therefore my heart is glad and my glory rejoices; my flesh also will dwell securely.
PSALM 16:8–9 NASB

When you make the conscious effort of keeping God continually before you, at your right hand, nothing in life will stress you. No loss or sorrow, no urgency or attack, no person, place, or material thing will shake you. That's what will give you joy in your heart and give you the security you need to live as God would have you live and to calmly and gladly do the tasks He has set before you, the ones that delight Him.

Keep the Lord close, and let all else be. With God, you can have that peace beyond understanding or surpassing.

Lord, I'm putting out my hand and drawing You close. Ah, what peace!

WAIT FOR IT

Therefore lift your drooping hands and strengthen your weak knees, and make straight paths for your feet. . . . That no one is . . .unholy like Esau, who sold his birthright for a single meal.
HEBREWS 12:12–13, 16 ESV

Esau allowed his hunger to lead him into a rash decision. He sold his birthright to his brother for some soup! Talk about overpaying for convenience. Esau's poor choice is a warning to the rest of us not to trade our future inheritance for momentary pleasures. So, when you feel weary of doing the right thing, when you've lost your eternal focus, lift your drooping hands and remember Esau! Don't sell out your eternal rewards for a fleeting moment of comfort.

Father, I know what I do here matters. When I'm tempted, help me to think about my eternity. Amen.

GOD BRINGS YOU TO A PLACE OF ABUNDANCE

*We went through fire and through water, but You brought us out
into a broad, moist place [to abundance and refreshment and
the open air]. . . . He brought me forth also into a large place
. . .because He was pleased with me and delighted in me.*
PSALM 66:12; 18:19 AMPC

Life is not without its trials, sticky situations, and happenings
that appear to be catastrophic at times. Yet while you're in those
places, you can be sure God is with you, shielding, comforting,
strengthening, and preparing to rescue you. He *will* pluck you
out and gently set you down in a broad place, one that's wide
enough for your feet to stand secure upon.

God is keen to deliver you because He's not only pleased but
delighted with you. He loves your face, form, smile, generosity,
and quirky sense of humor, your joy of life in Him. So no matter
what's going on in your life, breathe easy. God *will* bring you out
into the open air.

*Sometimes, Lord, I feel as if I'm drowning. Help me remember that
no matter where I am, You are with me and will soon pluck me out
of trouble and lead me to a place where I can breathe once more!*

WALK STRAIGHT IN HIS PURPOSE

For this very reason, make every effort to add to your faith goodness; and to goodness, knowledge; and to knowledge, self-control; and to self-control, perseverance; and to perseverance, godliness; and to godliness, mutual affection; and to mutual affection, love. . . . For if you do these things, you will never stumble, and you will receive a rich welcome into the eternal kingdom of our Lord and Savior Jesus Christ.
2 PETER 1:5–7, 10–11 NIV

Kids mimic our behavior, sometimes in heartbreaking detail. Likewise, those who are young in their faith are watching our example of what it looks like to follow Jesus.

Believing in Jesus isn't the end of your faith—it's the beginning of a journey. Have you added goodness, knowledge, self-control, perseverance, godliness, and love to your faith? Or are you staggering in sin?

Children are watching, so walk upright and turn from sin that they too will learn to walk correctly. Be an overcomer in God's plans for you here, and your welcome into God's kingdom will be rich!

Lord, keep my feet from stumbling. Amen.

GOD DAILY BEARS
YOUR BURDENS

*Blessed be the Lord, Who bears our burdens and carries
us day by day, even the God Who is our salvation!
Selah [pause, and calmly think of that]!*
PSALM 68:19 AMPC

It's so easy to take things for granted—the food you eat each
day, the home that shelters you from the storm, the car that
safely takes you to work, the dog who wags its tail whenever you
come through the door, the water that flows through your
spigot, the friends that provide endless support. . . The list goes
on and on!

Yet God not only provides for you, carrying you safely through
each day, but He also bears your burdens! Keep this in mind
today and every day. Lift up your voice in praise and gratitude
to Father God for the care, protection, and burdens He provides.
Blessed be the Lord!

*Thank You, Lord, for the way You take care of me every
single day, bearing my troubles, providing everything
I want and need, loving me, carrying me. My heart
overflows with love for You! You are an awesome God!*

LIVE IN POWER

*Crying out with a loud voice, he said, "What have you
to do with me, Jesus, Son of the Most High God?"*
MARK 5:7 ESV

Two demon-possessed men lived among the tombs. Scripture
says they were so violent that no one could subdue them or pass
that way. But the demons saw Jesus, and they recognized Him
immediately: "What have you to do with us, O Son of God? Have
you come here to torment us before the time?" (Matthew 8:29
ESV). They begged Jesus to send them into a herd of pigs, and
so He did.

The people who witnessed this were afraid. They didn't know
what to do with Jesus, so they told Him to go.

Have you ever been afraid of having Jesus in your life? You
don't know what to do with His power, so you ask Him to leave?

Instead of running from the power of Jesus, embrace the Son
of God. Tell Him you long for a real encounter with His power.

*Jesus, I give my life over to Your power.
Do with it what You will. Amen.*

GOD GUARDS YOUR HEART AND MIND

Don't worry about anything; instead, pray about everything.
Tell God what you need, and thank him for all he has
done. Then you will experience God's peace, which
exceeds anything we can understand. His peace will guard
your hearts and minds as you live in Christ Jesus.

PHILIPPIANS 4:6–7 NLT

There are so many things you don't have control over—people, events, organizations, governments, weather, and sometimes even your very self. That's why the apostle Paul tells you to hand everything over to God, the one who *does* have control over absolutely everything.

After you tell God all your concerns and things that you need, don't forget to thank Him. It's only then that you'll feel His peace come over you. You'll then enter into your day or close out your night with a heart that is supernaturally calm and a mind that's settled, enabling you to focus on and see what God would have you do and say.

I don't want to leave this place until I've handed all my
concerns over to You, Lord. Take these burdens, good
God. Please provide these needs. Thank You for all You
have done above and beyond my expectations.

Day 343
YOU LOVED ME FIRST

We love because he first loved us. If anyone says, "I love God,"
and hates his brother, he is a liar; for he who does not love his
brother whom he has seen cannot love God whom he has not seen.
1 JOHN 4:19 20 ESV

Beloved, you have a Father in heaven who eagerly anticipated your birth. He lovingly planned out the days of your life at the beginning of time. And He's been waiting for you ever since. He set in motion His great rescue, to send His own Son to die for you, so He'd never have to be parted from you again. He did all of this simply because He loved you first.

Love someone today.

Heavenly Father, I stand in the light of Your love—love I did
nothing to earn. You just gave it freely. I love You in return. Amen.

Day 344

GOD WANTS YOUR ATTENTION

*Eli told Samuel, "Go and lie down, and if he calls you, say, 'Speak, L*ORD*, for your servant is listening.' " So Samuel went and lay down in his place. The L*ORD *came and stood there, calling as at the other times, "Samuel! Samuel!" Then Samuel said, "Speak, for your servant is listening."*
1 SAMUEL 3:9–10 NIV

In those daily quiet moments, when, in that special place, you come before God in prayer, surrendered to His will and open to His way, say, "Speak, Lord. Your servant is listening." Then actually wait. Listen. Expect God to speak, to tell you that day's message. And in that silence, you will hear His voice. It may be a Bible verse that has touched your heart or the refrain of a hymn or worship song He wants you to take note of. The point is: keep your line of communication open between heaven and earth.

Here I am, Lord. Speak. Your servant is listening.
Convey Your message to my open heart and
willing spirit as I silently wait before You.

Day 345
HE'S HERE

"I've made myself available to those who haven't bothered to ask.
I'm here, ready to be found by those who haven't bothered
to look. I kept saying 'I'm here, I'm right here' to a nation
that ignored me. I reached out day after day to a people
who turned their backs on me, people who make wrong
turns, who insist on doing things their own way."
ISAIAH 65:1–2 MSG

Your heavenly Father longs for you to find Him. He aches for
your company. Whether you've sought Him or ignored Him,
whether you've messed up, whether you've been hurt or been
the source of hurt for others, or whether you've tried to do it all
on your own, He's holding out His hand. He's there. . .waiting. . .
for you. Will you reach out to Him before it's too late?

Father, thank You for reaching for me, for being
present and seeking. Thank You for knocking
on my door until I opened it. Amen.

GOD'S SPIRIT STRENGTHENS YOUR INNER WOMAN

*May He grant you out of the rich treasury of His
glory to be strengthened and reinforced with mighty
power in the inner man by the [Holy] Spirit [Himself
indwelling your innermost being and personality].*

Ephesians 3:16 ampc

When you determine to study God's Word, understand it, and live by it, your inner woman—your soul, spirit, mind, and personality— becomes stronger and stronger. You then have the unlimited power to live in hope, faith, and love and to do all that God is calling you to do without fainting or fearing.

This prayer of Paul's for yesterday's believers applies to you today. It reminds you of God's divine power that has its seat in and affects your entire inner life. Be cognizant of this unlimited strengthening and reinforcing power of God, knowing that God continues to supply it through His Spirit to your very core.

*All the strength You have given me, Lord, constantly
amazes me. Help me be more and more conscious of
the unlimited power that dwells so deep within me.*

Day 347
KNOWN

God, investigate my life; get all the facts firsthand. I'm an open
book to you; even from a distance, you know what I'm thinking.
You know when I leave and when I get back; I'm never out of
your sight. You know everything I'm going to say before I start the
first sentence. I look behind me and you're there, then up ahead
and you're there, too—your reassuring presence, coming and
going. This is too much, too wonderful—I can't take it all in!
PSALM 139:1–6 MSG

Loved one, do you find yourself in need of a friend, someone
who knows both your light and your darkness yet wants you
just the same? Someone who understands your history and the
varied motivations behind your every thought and action? If
you're looking for
    acceptance,
    relationship,
    friendship, and
    love. . .
Come to Jesus. He already knows *everything*. And He loves
you without condition.

Jesus, thank You for being my friend.
Help me be that kind of friend to others. Amen.

Day 348

GOD DOES FOR YOU MORE THAN YOU CAN IMAGINE

Now to Him Who, by (in consequence of) the [action of His] power that is at work within us, is able to [carry out His purpose and] do superabundantly, far over and above all that we [dare] ask or think [infinitely beyond our highest prayers, desires, thoughts, hopes, or dreams]—to Him be glory.
EPHESIANS 3:20–21 AMPC

Christ came into your heart when you accepted Jesus. But He's most at home in those hearts that are dedicated to Him. Those hearts that are "rooted deep in love and founded *securely* on love" (Ephesians 3:17 AMPC, emphasis added). The hearts that actually grasp the extent of God's love (see Ephesians 3:18), using the limitless supply of God's love to love others. For then they become flooded with "all the fullness of God" (Ephesians 3:19 AMPC).

God's unlimited power at work within you enables Him to do more than you ever imagined, hoped, or dreamed! He accomplishes things far beyond your highest prayers to Him!

I want to realize Your Spirit's strengthening of my inner being, Christ's immense love, and to be filled with You, Lord! Work in me beyond my dreams and hopes!

NEVER CAST OUT

"All that the Father gives me will come to me, and whoever comes to me I will never cast out. . . . For this is the will of my Father, that everyone who looks on the Son and believes in him should have eternal life, and I will raise him up on the last day."
JOHN 6:37, 40 ESV

Our friends and even our families are not always gentle with our hurts and shortcomings, and they're not always gracious in their welcome. Maybe you've struggled to fit in and never found acceptance. If so, don't despair in your loneliness, because there's hope!

God has a special you-shaped spot in His heart, and your place in His family can't be filled by any other. He loves you as His beloved daughter. Come to Him today. Experience His abundant grace and generous acceptance. He won't turn you away or tear you down, and He is always gentle and kind. He'll take you as you are.

Father, I'm coming home to Your presence.
Your marvelous grace has drawn me in. Amen.

GOD REWARDS YOUR PERSISTENT PRAYERS

Elijah. . .bowed low to the ground and prayed with his face between his knees. Then he said to his servant, "Go and look out toward the sea." The servant went and looked, then returned to Elijah and said, "I didn't see anything." Seven times Elijah told him to go and look.
1 KINGS 18:42–43 NLT

God had just instantly answered Elijah's prayer, sending down fire to burn up water-soaked wood (see 1 Kings 18:37–39). Now Elijah was telling King Ahab, "Go get something to eat and drink, for I hear a mighty rainstorm coming!" (1 Kings 18:41 NLT). Those were faith-filled words, considering it hadn't rained in Israel for three years!

God *will* grant your petitions either sooner or later, so don't give up! Remember, the vision will be fulfilled. "If it seems slow in coming, wait patiently, for it will surely take place" (Habakkuk 2:3 NLT).

Lord, help me be a patient and persistent prayer, filled with faith that You will fulfill my expectations. In You I need never give up!

NOT YOUR OWN

Or do you not know that your body is a temple of the Holy Spirit within you, whom you have from God? You are not your own, for you were bought with a price. So glorify God in your body.
1 Corinthians 6:19–20 esv

We tend to be a habit-driven bunch. And the habits of sin are so hard to break. Just when we begin to think we've arrived at maturity, we're blindsided by another misstep.

We grieve God when we choose sin over doing what is right, because we are His. We were bought at a staggeringly dear cost— the price was a precious and perfect life.

But where is our gratitude when we fail to change our ways after Jesus paid our impossible debt? Beloved, your body is His temple. You are not your own because you belong to someone greater. Glorify Him today.

Jesus, because of You I have a future of hope instead of despair and death. Give me strength to resist temptation. Amen.

Day 352

GOD WILL MEET YOU
WHERE YOU ARE

As he was sleeping, an angel touched him and told him,
"Get up and eat!" . . . Then the angel of the Lord came
again and touched him and said, "Get up and eat some
more, or the journey ahead will be too much for you."
1 Kings 19:5, 7 nlt

Elijah had just put the Baal prophets to shame after his God
answered his prayer. Then he prayed for rain—and it came. But
when Queen Jezebel threatened his life, Elijah, filled with fear,
took off. After a day's journey, he was so discouraged that he told
God to take his life. Then, exhausted, he fell asleep. But an angel
woke him, telling him to eat. Elijah discovered a warm cake of
bread and a jar of water. So he ate and drank then fell asleep,
only to be awakened and replenished by the angel a second time.

When, after mountaintop experiences, you're in the valley
of despair, God will replenish you until you can continue your
journey and once more hear His still, small voice.

Thank You, Lord, for meeting me where I am,
giving me what I need to go on my journey to You.

A REAL GEM

She opens her mouth with wisdom,
and the teaching of kindness is on her tongue.
PROVERBS 31:26 ESV

Wise and kind—no matter whether the Proverbs 31 woman encourages you or frustrates you, her legacy is something to emulate.

Bathe your mind in the wisdom and kindness of Jesus through His Word because when you're thinking with His mind, you can leave every conversation guilt-free. If you're not sure whether to let the words you're about to speak slip from your tongue, ask yourself, *Are they wise? Are they kind?* If not, it's best to do a quick rewrite of your dialogue before you open your mouth.

When you're tempted to lead with a cutting comeback, stop. Speak life instead. Speak wisdom and kindness. Your worth will be greater than diamonds.

Lord Jesus, fill my mouth with Your words.
Make me more and more like You so that my
words show Your love in all occasions. Amen.

GOD COMES THROUGH ON HIS PROMISES TO YOU

"God is not a man, so he does not lie. He is not human, so he does not change his mind. Has he ever spoken and failed to act? Has he ever promised and not carried it through?"
NUMBERS 23:19 NLT

Your God, who vows He'll never leave or forsake you (see Deuteronomy 31:6, 8), continues to keep His promises through Jesus who said, "And be sure of this: I am with you always, even to the end of the age" (Matthew 28:20 NLT).

To build up your faith and realize how much you matter to God, make a list of all God's promises. Then claim them one by one, following the advice of Hebrews 10:23 (NLT): "Let us hold tightly without wavering to the hope we affirm, for God can be trusted to keep his promise."

Lord, in a world where no one seems to be true to his word, I know I can count on You to keep Your promises to me. And in them I put all my hope!

Day 355
NUMBER YOUR DAYS

So teach us to number our days that
we may get a heart of wisdom.
PSALM 90:12 ESV

Psalms reminds us that our days here are few, and you only get this one chance at living—so make it count! Live by God's priorities. Don't lose sight of His plans amid the distractions of life.

What does this look like in today's chaotic world? It means not falling for the illusion that your life will never end. That things will slow down later—after your kids grow up or after you retire. God has plans for you today, in the life you're living now. Tomorrow might be too late. And He promises you a heart of wisdom when you begin to evaluate your priorities on an eternal scale. So live for God, for His glory, and for the increase of His kingdom. Do it today!

Lord, teach me to use my time wisely—for You. Amen.

Day 356

GOD GIVES BACK
WHAT YOU GIVE OUT

*Give, and [gifts] will be given to you; good measure, pressed down,
shaken together, and running over, will they pour into [the pouch
formed by] the bosom [of your robe and used as a bag]. For with
the measure you deal out [with the measure you use when you
confer benefits on others], it will be measured back to you.*
LUKE 6:38 AMPC

When Peter tells Jesus that they'd left their homes to follow Him,
Jesus replied, "No one who has sacrificed home, spouse, brothers
and sisters, parents, children—whatever—will lose out. It will
all come back multiplied many times over in your lifetime. And
then the bonus of eternal life!" (Luke 18:29–30 MSG).

It works the same way with what money you offer to God.
When you bring all your tithes into the storehouse, God says,
"I will open the windows of heaven for you. I will pour out a
blessing so great you won't have enough room to take it in! Try
it! Put me to the test!" (Malachi 3:10 NLT).

*You're so generous to me, Lord, spurring me on to
give and give, knowing You'll keep me in the black!*

HOPE FOR THE WEARY

*"I [fully] satisfy the weary soul, and I replenish
every languishing and sorrowful person."*
JEREMIAH 31:25 AMP

Sin often looks so much easier than doing the right thing. Easier
sounds better than serving. And it certainly sounds better than
denying ourselves and hefting a heavy cross to follow Jesus.

Jesus didn't promise us an easy life, but neither did He leave
us here on earth alone with our battles to be beaten down by
inevitable burnout. Instead He said, "Come to me, all who labor
and are heavy laden, and I will give you rest" (Matthew 11:28 ESV).

If you're living in a bleary-eyed fog, anxious and fearful
about your tomorrows or if suffering and sorrow sear your heart,
your burdens belong to Him. Come. Trust in His goodness. Be
replenished.

*Jesus, thank You for restoring my strength and refreshing
my perspective. You patiently provide for all my needs—
physical, emotional, and spiritual. Please help me deal kindly
with others when they too need refreshment. Amen.*

GOD SHINES HIS PRESENCE UPON YOU

The Lord bless you and watch, guard, and keep you;
the Lord make His face to shine upon and enlighten you
and be gracious (kind, merciful, and giving favor) to you;
the Lord lift up His [approving] countenance upon you and
give you peace (tranquility of heart and life continually).
NUMBERS 6:24–26 AMPC

God loves to bless you, giving you all you need to live and more, including His very presence. He wants you to know He and His angels are watching over you, guarding and protecting you. God is smiling down upon you; His presence is like a ray of sunshine, giving you love and light for your path. He longs to be kind to you and favor you. He does see you, notice you, and treat you as a favored daughter. And the peace He covers you with is not just serenity in the time of trouble but a feeling of total well-being.

Precious daughter, claim this blessing from your loving God for you matter to Him.

Lord, You are the sunshine that brightens up my life,
lifts my spirit, and makes me whole. Thank You for
loving me more than any other. I praise Your name!

Day 359

GOD DOES THE WORK

When the poor and needy seek water, and there is none, and their tongue is parched with thirst, I the LORD will answer them; I the God of Israel will not forsake them. I will open rivers on the bare heights, and fountains in the midst of the valleys. I will make the wilderness a pool of water, and the dry land springs of water. . . . That they may see and know, may consider and understand together, that the hand of the LORD has done this, the Holy One of Israel has created it.
ISAIAH 41:17–18, 20 ESV

It often takes a problem we can't fix for us to admit our own limits and learn to trust God. When we're trying to do God's job of holding the universe together, He often seems to step back and let us have a go at it. And then He gently asks, "Are you finished now?"

In His wisdom He knows our egos will most likely take credit for His work if He steps in too soon. So He patiently waits until we realize that we need Him, that we're spent and empty. That when all our resources have been used up, God remains.

Lord, help me to rely on You and not my own strength. Amen.

Day 360

NAMED

You shall be called by a new name that
the mouth of the Lord will give.
ISAIAH 62:2 ESV

Our greatest enemy is a liar. Yep, he's a big, fat fibber. Don't ever forget it. When he tells you that you're unworthy, unwanted, unloved, hopeless, or forgotten, you can look him in the eye and say, "Not true!" If he tells you that your name is Nothing, don't buy it. He's bluffing, beloved.

God has given you a new name. He calls you. . .
cherished,
loved,
known,
forgiven,
accepted, and
beautiful.
He is yours, and you are His beloved. You belong to Him.

Father, You have called me Yours. You have renamed me
and claimed me. Help me recognize the accusations of Satan
for what they are—lies. Help me find my worth in who You
created me to be. . .in who You say that I am. Amen.

Day 361

BECAUSE YOU
BELONG TO HIM. . .

"If they made it very hard for Me, they will make it very hard
for you also. If they obeyed My teachings, they will obey your
teachings also. They will do all these things to you because you
belong to Me. They do not know My Father Who sent Me."
John 15:20–21 nlv

Through the tough times, when you're being trampled by a
world that has rejected Jesus, remember that you won't re
ceive better treatment in this fallen place than Jesus did. But
there is hope! Jesus warned us of the difficulties so we wouldn't
be easily discouraged by the severe hardship we might experience in this world. But your hope rests in *who* you belong to.
Don't be swayed by popular culture's mocking voice. Heaven
awaits!

Father, someday when I'm with You in eternity, I know
the trials of this world will seem like an insignificant blink.
Give me strength to endure. In Jesus' name, amen.

Day 362

CLING TO HIM

*"You shall follow the Lord your God and fear Him;
and you shall keep His commandments, listen to
His voice, serve Him, and cling to Him."*
Deuteronomy 13:4 nasb

In a "take charge of your destiny" world, trusting God can be a hard sell. It's vital to keep our perspective in check. When we're shopping online for a new pair of boots, we read every review to discover their performance in all types of weather. And God doesn't ask us to trust Him blindly without evidence either. The Bible is loaded with positive reviews from faithful people who chose to follow His leading, even when things weren't looking so good. Allow God to lead, even in your mess, and listen for His voice. Never let go of the one who sees both ends of eternity.

Father, teach me to trust You more. In Jesus' name, amen.

SAFE HOUSE

*God's a safe-house for the battered, a sanctuary
during bad times. The moment you arrive,
you relax; you're never sorry you knocked.*
PSALM 9:9–10 MSG

Have you ever gone through bad times? Maybe you're feeling battered by life right now—as if you were chosen only to struggle and never to thrive. Friend, whether it's an illness, a wayward child, financial struggles, or anxiety, you can find hope, help, and shelter in your heavenly Father. As the scripture says, the moment you arrive in His presence, you'll relax. He may not remove all your problems, but He'll change and strengthen you through them. Go to Him in prayer. Find Him in His Word. Trust Him, and He will never forsake you.

*Father, I need a place of shelter, a safe place
to rest my anxiety-burdened mind. I'm chosen
to thrive in this dry place. Amen.*

Day 364

ALL I EVER WANTED

He fulfills the desires of those who fear him;
he hears their cry and saves them.
PSALM 145:19 NIV

Have you asked God for things and He hasn't delivered? You may think that He isn't listening, doesn't care, or just can't help you. But maybe it's something else altogether. Maybe the things you're asking for aren't good for your soul, or perhaps you need to take a hard look at your motives for asking. Are they selfish? The more we get to know God the more His desires become our desires. And when what you want lines up with what God wants, you'll hear a lot more "Yes!" from your heavenly Father.

Lord, change my heart, soften it, and remove the hard
core of selfishness that often has me thinking of my
own comfort and pleasure. Help me see the needs of
others. Help me see their need for You. Amen.

Day 365

CHOSEN TO HOPE

*"I have come as Light into the world, so that everyone
who believes in Me will not remain in darkness."*
JOHN 12:46 NASB

Hope is born! And we desperately need it. The message of Jesus'
birth is not just one for the Christmas season. Friend, no matter
what difficult or desperate circumstances you're facing, Jesus
offers hope. He doesn't promise a perfect, comfortable life or
that you'll get everything you want. Instead, He offers Himself as
your hope—the light that pierces the dark. Hope that you have a
loving Savior who died to take away the burden of your sin. Hope
that God works even the hard things together for our ultimate
good when we walk in His ways.

*Father, thank You for the precious gift of hope. I know
that Your plan for me is good, my sins are forgiven,
and I will live with You forever in heaven. Amen.*

SCRIPTURE INDEX

MORE INSPIRATION FOR YOUR LOVELY HEART

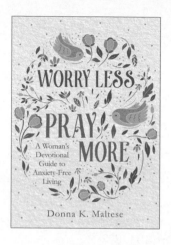

Worry Less, Pray More

This purposeful devotional guide features 180 readings and prayers designed to help alleviate your worries as you learn to live in the peace of the Almighty God, who offers calm for your anxiety-filled soul. *Worry Less, Pray More* reinforces the truth that, with God, you can live anxiety-free every single day—whether you worry about your work, relationships, bills, the turmoil of the world, or something more.

Paperback / 978-1-68322-861-5